CHRIS KNOPF

YOU'RE DEAD

THE PERMANENT PRESS
Sag Harbor, NY 11963

For information, address:
The Permanent Press
4170 Noyac Road
Sag Harbor, NY 11963
www.thepermanentpress.com

Library of Congress Cataloging-in-Publication Data

Knopf, Chris, author.
  You're dead / Chris Knopf.
  Other titles: You are dead
  Sag Harbor, NY: Permanent Press, [2018]
  ISBN: 978-1-57962-566-5
    1. Mystery fiction.

PS3611.N66 Y68 2018
813'.6—dc23   2018039060

Printed in the United States of America

CHAPTER ONE

There was something about my relationship with dead weight that enlivened me.

I could bench press 340 pounds and so far hadn't ruptured any ligaments or snapped any bones. None of the people in the weight room felt the need to socialize, much less directly compete, which we all knew would spoil the mood. So we stayed in our private lanes, unless spotting for each other, a frequent responsibility gladly shared. Otherwise, we were all independent, self-contained entities with rock-hard bodies and minimal social ambitions. People who grunted and stank, and kept their own counsel.

After the workout, if the spirit moved me, and it usually did, I'd go from the gym to a nearby joint called Skinny McDowell's. An American reimagining of an Irish pub, it was dark, with worn woodwork, booths with uncomfortable backrests, Irish flags, and Guinness on tap. A diverse group of regulars clustered around the bar—professional people, working stiffs, a couple academics, a retired fire chief, and me, bound only by being single men with a taste for booze and easy company.

The fire chief, a professor, and the owner of an auto repair shop were eating when I got there. The bartender brought my usual Guinness, and without bothering to ask, put in an order of cobb salad.

Known by the habits you keep.

Professor Bowdin was likely on his fourth Bourbon on the rocks, ramping up to a limit of six, after which his precise eloquence would evaporate and one of us would have to drive him home. Usually the fire chief, who stuck with nonalcoholic O'Doul's, claiming a tendency to start punching people after the first sip of regular beer.

The wonders of human capacity.

"I was hoping you'd come in, being the shrink-in-residence around here," said the mechanic. "We're debating. Are people born evil, or just made that way by life circumstances?"

"That's too big a question for a quick answer," I told them.

"That's been my position," said Bowdin.

It was a question people spent a lot of time thinking about, ever since they started calling psychology a science— arguing with colleagues, writing papers, pontificating at conferences. I had an answer for them, but probably not what they hoped for.

"Both," I said, as my salad appeared in front of me.

"Hah!" said Bowdin. "The enigmatic Dr. Waters."

"What do enemas got to do with it?" asked the chief.

The mechanic grinned at that, and they traded high fives.

"Or neither," I said. "It's an empty argument. Unless you're in some meaningless academic debate, no offense, Professor, it will do nothing to alter, convert, or overcome the evildoer."

I took a big forkful of my salad.

"I think you have your answer," said Bowdin.

"An SOB is an SOB, however he got there," said the mechanic.

"Or she," I said.

Bowdin, a linguistics professor, applauded expanding the definition.

"Sometimes the bitch herself is the problem," he said. "Not her son."

"Any other existential quandaries you philosophers want figured out?" I asked.

Bowdin peered into his glass.

"Why is this thing always half-empty? Where does the other half go?"

———— • ————

I LIVED in a condo that was an apartment until I got a letter saying I could give the building owner a five thousand dollar down payment and turn my rent, slightly reduced, into a mortgage. Not a hard decision, though I often wondered if I really liked the place enough to actually own it.

When I got there that night, the front door was open. The lamp in the living room was on, triggered by an automatic timer. I listened for any sounds, but it was quiet. Before I moved away from the door, I pulled the lampshade off the sturdy little table lamp and yanked out the cord. Holding the lamp like a club, I moved around the condo, but found nothing else out of the ordinary.

Until I walked into the spare bedroom and saw the head of Paresh Rajput, the owner of my company, ExciteAble Technologies, in the center of a small lake of dark red blood.

I staggered into the guest bathroom and stared into the mirror above the sink, then heaved my guts out, until all that was left was a wracking cough.

I washed my face and went back to the guest room where I slid down behind the bed in a way that blocked the head from my line of sight. I sat on the floor and cleared the choke hold on my throat before calling the police.

I occasionally worked as a consultant for Andy Pettigrew, the New Haven police department's forensic psychologist, for extra money, but more importantly, it was a way to spend time in a world as far from the concerns of aerospace manufacturing, as the moons circling Jupiter.

The work mostly involved fitness evaluations of rookie cops coming in, cops after a shooting or particularly tough arrest, cops starting to splinter after too much time on high stress assignments, cops who needed to get off the street, but just didn't know it yet. Pettigrew did all the interviews and field work; I just sat around with him providing fresh eyes and ears.

Occasionally, though rarely, the detectives would run into a tricky interrogation, and brought Pettigrew in to watch the monitor, or even join them in the room. I got to play in that sand box, too, a few times, and got to breathe the same air as some fairly serious sons of bitches. Since I'd once dealt with my share of sons of bitches, serious and otherwise, Pettigrew liked having my point of view.

This time it was me in the chair facing the video camera and Pettigrew with his detective colleagues on the other side of the table. I spent four hours explaining to them what I knew about Paresh Rajput's head ending up in my guest bedroom, which was nothing. The detectives, led by an intense guy named Noah Shapiro, pressed me hard on possible enemies of Paresh or any other aggressive types that might have a grudge. I gave them a short list of the bad actors I'd helped sweep out of the company. Once they were gone, the men and women I worked with at the plant were on the whole amiable and good-natured people. They were highly skilled technical experts who configured and optimized the machines that built intricate parts for the aviation industry. Engineers, programmers, machinists, and hardware specialists. Thoughtful, mostly reserved people focused on their difficult work. Though given the importance of teamwork and collaboration, I fostered a sense of camaraderie by managing the group dynamics, which included careful screening at the hiring stage, filtering out the contentious and unruly.

As congenial as these relationships were, they stopped at the door. I knew virtually nothing about their private lives, referring those who came to me with personal issues to human resources, who had a psychologist of their own on retainer. The last time I practiced individual therapy was in graduate school, since a year of it was required to earn a PhD. My work with the police force was confined to consulting with Pettigrew, who subsequently worked directly with the cops.

After leaving the police station, I checked into a residence hotel, leaving the CSIs and homicide detectives to their work at my condo. I stripped down to my boxers, drank a few beers, and spent some time on my laptop, looking around the Internet for news of other beheadings, until hobbled by the need to sleep.

I lay faceup on top of the bedspread, and thought about the loss of Paresh, someone I cared about more than I knew until the man was irretrievably taken away. The loss squeezed my heart, until fantasies of escape, learned in childhood to ward off demons, gave enough relief to allow me to slide into a dream-tormented sleep.

When I got to the company in the morning, my assistant, Joey Adams, met me at the main entrance. He had jet-black hair and a beard to match, which made his face look even more unusually pale.

"How is everybody?" I asked him.

"You mean the ones who showed up for work? Somewhere between inconsolably grief-stricken and freaking terrified."

I asked where he fell on that scale.

"About midway, but I like compromise."

He said Megan Rajput, Paresh's Irish-American wife, was waiting for me in the main conference room. Megan was ten years younger than Paresh and nuttier by many orders of magnitude. She'd been the company's first employee, handling the books on the kitchen table while he spent days and nights in the basement cranking out prototypes. I liked her, despite her tendency to blurt out inappropriate comments at social events and more than once stuff her tongue in my mouth in the midst of a good-bye kiss.

Before I went to see her, I asked Joey to tell human resources to bring in a team of disaster counselors.

"They need to drop everything and do it immediately," I said. "Get a big team. Minimum wait times. And I want uniformed security at every entrance. With plainclothes people walking the halls. Get the word out now. Tell employees what we're doing. Send out an e-mail from me."

He told me facilities management was in charge of security.

"So call the outside security people directly," I said. "The biggest, baddest bastards you can find. Tell facilities to shut up and cooperate, in that diplomatic way you have."

"I thought you were the diplomacy expert around here."

"Not today. We also need a company-wide meeting."

I told him to put the memo out on Fred Warner's letterhead, our chief of engineering and number two in the company. Joey looked worried about that, but I told him Fred was flying in from Wichita and it couldn't wait for him to get back.

"What are you going to tell the employees?" he asked.

"I don't know yet. I guess I'll ask the new owner."

Megan was the only one in the big conference room, sitting at the head of the table. She was wearing a sweatshirt and her hair was tied in a ponytail. Her head was lowered, and she was sobbing. I cleared my throat.

"Waters," she croaked out. "Oh my God."

"I'm sorry, Megan," was all I could think to say.

I walked down the length of the table and met her as she stood up to hug. It was a fiercely strong hug.

"I don't know what to do," she said. "I can't think. My mind has disappeared."

"Anybody's would," I said, holding on for a bit, then gently extracting myself from her arms.

"The police won't tell me anything," she said. "Who would do this? Who's next?"

She raised a question I hadn't asked myself. Had the killer started at the top with the intention of working his way down the chain of command? I used my smartphone to call Joey and have him add personal bodyguards for Megan and Fred Warner to the security detail. The bodyguard should meet Fred at the airport. As I spoke, Megan's face steadily filled with dread.

"You don't really think," she started to say, after I hung up with Joey.

"I don't. But it's crucial for the employees to regain their sense of stability and security. Meanwhile, it can't hurt to have some protection around the place. Because, honestly, nobody knows for sure."

I also told her about the disaster counselors and the need for a company-wide meeting. I started to suggest what we should say when she laid her hand on my arm and told me the board of directors had put me on paid leave and wanted me to stay away from the plant and its employees.

"They spoke to the police, who apparently told them more than they'd tell me. And here you are working so hard to help us all through this," she said.

I said I understood. I'd do the same thing if I was in their position. The company's CEO was found dead in an employee's condominium. Have to suspend the guy. No hard feelings.

"I don't want you to go, but I can't fight with the board right now," she said.

"You can't."

Megan dug her pale Irish face, crushed by exhaustion, into my chest.

"Oh God, oh God, oh God."

I held her again and said I'd get Colin Brice, our CFO and next in line after Fred Warner, to come stay with her and help plot out future steps. Face still nuzzled, she shook her head, but said okay.

I had to let her go so I could get to my office for the first time that morning.

"Waters," she said, before I could make it all the way out the door. "I know how much Paresh meant to you. I really do. It's okay to let yourself grieve."

"I'm already there, Megan," I said. "More than you know. But we have to keep this place together. And stay focused on the primary goal."

"What's that?"

"Putting the bastard who did this in the ground."

Chapter Two

When I got to my office the phone was ringing. I dropped my briefcase on the conference table and snatched it off the cradle.

"You're dead" said a robotic voice, a male voice, mechanized and unmodulated.

"Who are you?"

"Your killer."

Then he hung up.

I hit the call back function, but the window confirmed the number was unavailable. I called the company's IT manager.

"Can you get the number of a call that just came in on my direct line?" I asked her. "The phone said it was unknown."

"Unlikely," she said, "but I can try."

A few minutes later she called back to state the obvious. No way.

"What sort of call was it?" she asked.

"Nothing important," I said. "Just curious."

I hung up, then stared at the phone for a few moments. When it didn't ring again, I got up to go get a cup of coffee, not knowing what else to do.

When I got back to the office, the message light on the phone was blinking. I picked it up.

"Not everyone gets notified of their impending death," said the mechanical voice. Then the caller hung up and someone knocked on my door. I jumped a little in my seat, but it was Joey Adams.

"Just checking in," he said. "You okay?"

"I've been better."

"You don't look too good. Can hardly blame you."

I shook my head.

"I'm okay. What do we got?"

"Just the company meeting," he said.

"I won't be there."

"You won't?"

"I'm on leave. Board decision. I'm off premises until the cops clear me. It's a formality."

"Not to me," said Joey. "That's ridiculous."

"I have to make a call, then I'm taking off."

Joey was a young, energetic guy, given to an excess of enthusiasm, which I could hardly count as a sin. He rarely looked bothered by anything, though that day he looked ready to hurl himself out a window.

"You know how much work we have?" he asked.

"I'll call you in a day or two. We'll figure it out."

When he left the office, I called Andy Pettigrew and told him about the phone calls and the failed attempt at tracing them.

"Your tech is probably right about that," said Pettigrew.

"Maybe Megan was also right," I said, sharing her comment, *Who's next?*

"There's some logic to knocking off the CEO, but why you?" Pettigrew asked.

"Not a clue. I'm just a company man. I work with management, screen candidates, train people, coach work teams.

I eat, sleep, work out, and hang around in bars. No time to make enemies."

"You think it's the same guy who killed Rajput?"

"Undoubtedly," I said. "If someone had it in for him, I sure didn't know about it. And I guess he has it in for me too. That actually should tell us something."

"You two met at the casino, right?"

"What's that got to do with it?" I asked.

"No sore losers?"

I knew what he meant. Before ExciteAble, I had a few good years playing poker, ending abruptly when I was met at the door of the casino by the head of security and two guys who stood with their hands in their pockets. I knew what was coming but pretended I didn't.

"Hi, fellas," I said. "How are the tables running?"

The security guy explained in flat, even tones that I was being banned from every gaming venue from Maine to Atlantic City.

"What the hell for?"

He told me they didn't know how I was doing it, but statistically, I was too good a poker player to win the way I did. Too steady, too consistent.

"We got a computer that tells us who's out of whack with the norms. We've had you on watch for a year. The gaming commission gave the okay. You're outta here."

"For winning too much?"

"No. For not losing."

Blame it on the arrogance of youth. I'd assumed if I didn't get greedy, kept a low profile, and walked away from the table before the bets got too high, I'd be ignored.

I must have looked panicky, because the two other guys moved in a little closer.

"You had a good run, buddy," said the security guy. "Go find something else to amuse yourself."

I had something else, which was why I needed those winnings, and why I rarely played past midnight. I had to get back to my dorm room to jam in some studying before my ten o'clock class.

"I wasn't cheating," I said. "I need the money."

"We all need money. Go get an honest job," he said, putting a hand on my shoulder to guide me out the door.

"I'll tell you how I did it," I said, rushing out the words. I felt his hand give a slight squeeze. "Don't you want to know? I won't play anymore. I just want to get paid for the information."

He gave me a hard look, but let his hand drop.

"That's a first," he said.

"You're a betting man. What do you got to lose?" I said.

He thought that was almost funny, but I knew I had him. So instead of getting marched out the door, he brought me through the casino and into the back rooms where management had their offices. I had to wait for a while, but eventually he had me sit down with a young Asian woman who ran the table games. She dismissed the security guy, which he didn't like, before saying to me, "I'm listening."

"Tells," I said to her.

Her hand drifted over to her phone, poised to call the security guy back in. But before she pushed the button, she said, "Seriously?"

Poker isn't really a game of chance. It's one of wit and deception. One of the few contests where a gambler can develop skills that overcome the random nature of card play. Beat the odds. Beat the other players around the table. Beat the house.

A key skill is reading "tells." The involuntary declarations of mood and intent written on people's faces and movements. The best players not only know how to obscure these reflex messages, but use them to their advantage. Though no one is entirely opaque. If you knew how to look.

"I can't tell you how I do it, but I can prove I'm not lying," I said. "Or cheating. Just give me the chance. I'll never play in your casino again, but I don't want to be banned."

She pushed a button on her phone, but instead of calling in security, she told her admin she'd be on the floor for a while.

"Come with me," she said.

I don't remember the particulars of the night, beyond walking around the tables and predicting how the players would play their hands. She was pretty good herself, but I had her about three to one. It all concluded with her offering me a job and promising to let the gaming commission know I was off the banned list.

"As long as you don't play here, which you can't anyway if we employ you."

The money wasn't as good, but the work a lot more interesting. My career tally for busting cheats was a dozen. Mostly card counters and a team of two from Carnegie Mellon with tiny two-way radios imbedded in their bodies. As time progressed, security found me useful for other types of work, principally bouncing drunks and other disorderly customers. With no professional hand-to-hand training, I just relied on a sort of vertical form of wrestling, a sport I excelled at in high school and college.

One fistfight I broke up resulted in a hospital stay for one of the combatants. A later investigation, supported by the security cams, determined I'd used appropriate force, though barely. I was young, and simply didn't know my own strength.

This was so long ago, and the guy was such a dope, he couldn't be the anonymous caller. Stupid just didn't seem to fit.

The most valuable outcome of my security gig was meeting Paresh Rajput, a serious player and friend of the Asian table games manager. He paid me a thousand dollars to tell him what he was signaling during his play. His game got a lot better, and I got a patron who paid for my last year of grad school and hired me the day I earned my degree.

"What do you want me to do?" I asked him.

"Watch my back."

As it turned out, I did everything but.

When I made it to the hotel, I didn't know what to do next, so almost by reflex I started sketching out a description of the killer:

>Male.
>Narcissistic.
>Delusional.
>Capable of carrying out extreme acts of violence.
>Intelligent.
>Resourceful.
>A deep planner.
>Bold.

If I was right about the narcissism, the guy would need to communicate, to sustain the ability to terrorize and illicit a response. So while the wait was frustrating, I knew it wouldn't last. And I was right.

"How are you enjoying things so far?" said the mechanical voice when I answered my smartphone.

I pushed the end button.

The phone rang again, and I ignored the ringing until it stopped. A few minutes later, it rang again, and I turned off the phone and tossed it over my shoulder.

Somehow Megan had persuaded the cops to keep the specifics of her husband's demise out of the news. It was bad enough that a local business owner had been found murdered in his staff psychologist's condominium. Though I suspected another issue was the missing headless body, something the cops would just as soon not have to explain. The article noted that the psychologist had not been named as a suspect, though expressed in a way that didn't eliminate the possibility.

My smartphone chirped an alert at me. Very unwelcomed, since it meant my latest bank statement was waiting for review. A hated exercise, even more so that morning, but I looked anyway.

Everything was in order except for my money market account, which had a balance of a hundred and twenty thousand dollars, all but twenty thousand of which I had no knowledge of. It had been deposited the day Paresh was killed.

I called Pettigrew and told him someone had dumped a pile of money in my bank account without my knowledge.

"You better come back in," he said. "And bring all your bank statements. Everything. Retirement accounts, investments, the works."

I did what he asked and was soon back in the interview room.

This time, the interviewers included a guy in a blue blazer, polo shirt, and wrinkled khakis. A forensic accountant. We were in the usual room where I was told to sit at a metal table and face a video camera mounted on the wall close to the ceiling. I asked for Pettigrew, but they said he was unavailable. I handed over all the documents I'd brought in, along with my tax returns for the last two years. For about an hour we sat around the table while the accountant went through it all, page by page, painfully scrutinizing and questioning every line item on every statement. Painful for me, obviously not for him.

"You say you have no idea where this deposit came from?" he finally asked me. He withdrew a sheet of paper from his briefcase. "I have the transaction record in front of me. Would you like to think again before I tell you?"

I wanted to think some more, but not about the deposit. More about what it implied. But I shook my head.

"It was a direct deposit from ExciteAble Technologies, the firm belonging to the late CEO, Paresh Rajput," said one of the homicide detectives. "Described in the general ledger as a bonus for the current calendar year."

I told him our bonuses always came as a check handed out at the Christmas party.

"Indeed," he said. "And last year you received one of the bigger checks. Paresh must have thought a lot of you."

"He did," I said.

"Of course," said the accountant.

We endured another half hour of watching him trace his finger across the statements and tax returns, until he finally raised his head again. He reached into his briefcase and pulled out another sheet of paper.

"Too bad you won't have your condo mortgage to write off again this year," he said.

"Why not?"

"It's paid in full. You'll probably get your letter from the bank today."

He handed me another document he slid out of his briefcase. It was from the mortgage company, discharging the loan. It was dated the day of Paresh's death.

"I didn't do it," I said.

A sudden stillness gripped the austere interview room. The accountant and two homicide detectives were fixed in place, their eyes trying hard to look into mine. It was then I knew the question I'd hear next.

"Pay off the mortgage or kill Rajput?" said one of the detectives, as he looked back at the one-way mirror and gave a thumbs-up.

CHAPTER THREE

When I was a kid, I didn't understand why my brother screamed and cried, and fought off my stepfather, who was trying to pull me into the car. Why he begged him and my mother not to take me away, promising that he knew how to make me better. Back then, such histrionics were as mysterious to me as the workings of subatomic particles, and the concept of "better," equally unfathomable.

My stepfather let go of my shirtsleeve, and sticking a finger nearly in my brother's face, yelled, "You get one week. That's it."

My mother just wept into her hands.

The first thing my brother taught me was to look people in the eye. He figured it was the only way he could convince my stepfather to stave off institutionalization for at least a few more weeks. None of it made any sense at the time, but his therapeutic approach, consisting of threats, bribes, and frequent smacks to the head, must have been effective, since a week passed and I was still in the house.

It was probably unsettling for people to engage with a twelve-year-old who stared unflinchingly into their eyes, but that's what I did, discovering that the way they stared back, or tried to evade my gaze, told me something about what they were thinking. I'm not sure how it evolved from there, but by the time I was thirteen, my brother was actively training me to read social cues and respond appropriately.

I didn't see this as training, but rather a type of deeply involving game. A secret game between us, where we'd have an encounter with another person, then safely in our bedroom, dissect what happened and what it all meant. Already obsessive, I took to the game with an all-consuming verve, which my brother patiently and tirelessly endured.

By fourteen, I was enrolled in regular high school, having made the transition from learning-disabled to gifted. To me, there was little difference. I'd always had a facility for concentration and memorization, I just hadn't seen the value in demonstrating this to the benighted adults charged with my care. But now I understood how living in the wider world enhanced the game, offering richer experiences to share and evaluate with my brother.

He never left my side except during school hours since he was two years ahead. Though younger, I was much bigger. The other kids called us Lenny and George, and we had a few ugly fights as a consequence, though it spread quickly that the Lenny part of the team was very difficult to subdue. And on the whole, we were well-liked, mostly because my brother was an extreme extrovert, witty and adept with the better-looking girls.

I studied everything he did, and how he did it. And followed his every instruction, reinforced by every success. With this came greater independence, and as we moved into our later teens, I became completely self-sufficient, which he encouraged. In fact, I was there when the school guidance counselor told my mother that I'd basically recovered, with just a few residual effects, something that only happened to less than a quarter of autistic kids. She said it was a miracle.

In my case, the miracle was my brother.

The lawyer's name was Jadeen Knox. A young, rail-thin product of Yale Law School who spent half her time, pro bono, on New Haven hard cases, and the other half representing people like me, who could pay her firm's breathtaking hourly fees. She'd plucked more than one hapless innocent out of the prosecutorial cauldron, earning a reputation that well exceeded her tenure as a defense attorney.

Andy Pettigrew strongly advised I give her a call after the cops let me know I was on their suspect list for Paresh's murder. In fact, the only one on the list.

I would have already been arrested if it weren't for an assortment of incongruities. What motive would I have to kill my boss, with whom, by all accounts, I had an excellent relationship? Why chop off his head and place it in my own condominium, then alert the police? Why would I voluntarily call attention to the hundred-thousand-dollar deposit? If it was extortion, why cut off the source?

And then there were the death threats. This shaped a story, fairly symmetrical, that it was all a big frame-up. Which seemed unlikely to the cops, but credible enough to hold back further proceedings. At least for the time being.

I learned all this from Pettigrew, who told me revealing this information could be construed as interfering with a police investigation, and thus grounds for dismissal, or possible prosecution.

"So you didn't hear it from me."

I thanked him and called Ms. Knox.

"You can call me Jadeen," she said, when we first talked on the phone.

"You can call me Waters," I said. "Everyone else does."

"How about Dr. Waters. You got the PhD."

"Just Waters is fine."

"Don't like your first name?"

"Never stuck."

Jadeen's office was in an ancient house in a neighborhood north of downtown New Haven that her partners had restored to historical and aesthetic perfection. The room had enough deep red mahogany to raise the ambient temperature and was so quiet I could hear my own breath. We sipped coffee from tiny teacups likely sourced from a dealer of Asian antiquities.

"You haven't been charged yet," she said, flipping through some paperwork. "So that's good."

"I shouldn't be. I didn't do it."

She held up both hands, as if warding off unwanted information.

"You don't have to tell me that."

"Yes, I do. I didn't do it," I said.

"Around here, we're big on presumed innocence."

"I'm not sure that's true."

Jadeen took off her glasses and looked up from the documents she was reading so she could send her angry gaze directly at me. That might have meant to be intimidating, which it sort of was.

"I believe all my clients," she said.

"No, you don't. You probably don't believe most of them. But I'm telling you the truth."

She tossed the file on her desk and doubled down on the fierce glower.

"You have no better chance at dodging this than me," she said.

"I'm not dodging anything. This is about a deranged bastard trying to ruin me, or ruin the company, or both. If you think anything else, you're no good to me. I'm sorry I'm a man, but I can't do anything about that."

She looked perplexed, but softened a little around the mouth.

"What's that got to do with it?"

"You distrust men. Probably with good reason. You have a portrait of your family on your credenza. Two kids. No father, but two mommies. You're well regarded and successful, but you didn't get there just by being smart and hard working. You've always had to out-compete or overcome some lunkheaded man who thought excess testosterone bequeathed some sort of divine right."

She gave me a long, slow looking over.

"You gonna be one of those kinds of clients, aren't you?" she said.

"I'm gonna be a great client. I have nothing but respect and admiration for you and will do everything you tell me to do. I just don't want to be treated like an idiot child."

She lightened further, almost to the point of letting a smile possess her face.

"I thought psychologists are supposed to be, like, these quiet, gentle guys in Harris Tweeds who make you feel all comfy and secure."

"I just want to move past the superiority games and get down to saving my ass, which I'm told you're uniquely qualified to do," I said to her.

I could see I'd struck the right chord with her, but it wasn't really a brilliant maneuver. It was an impulsive reaction to some real fear that was bubbling around the nether reaches of my brain, despite my best efforts to keep it down there.

She leaned forward at her desk and tapped a stack of papers in front of her.

"Okay, mind reader, what's up with *your* love life? A young man living by himself, with no known relationships?"

My first impulse was to lie, immediately violating my claim to be an excellent client. It was understandable, at least to me, given the agreement I had with my friend—with whom I had a rich romantic involvement—to never reveal our secret.

"I have someone. A female. We keep it under wraps."

"Married?"

"Yes."

"Can she provide an alibi?" she asked.

"No. So I hope we can keep her out of this."

"Even if it would save your ass, which you just reminded me is my job?"

"Hell no. My ass comes first."

That seemed to do the trick, and the rest of our first interview settled into professional discourse, if not overly warm and chummy. She outlined how she thought things would proceed with the cops. We agreed to cooperate wherever it made sense, but to discuss every disclosure before it was made. They'd already gone through my condo and had full access to my financial records. She told me to volunteer my car for the investigation before they had a chance to ask for it.

"And my storage unit," I said.

"You didn't tell me about that."

"I forgot about it. Haven't been there in months. It's almost empty."

My cell phone rang. I looked at the screen and told Jadeen it was the New Haven detective assigned to the case.

She said, "Go ahead and answer. Be cooperative. But put it on speaker."

"Detective Shapiro, this is Waters," I said. "Before you say anything, I want to give you my car to go over, as well as a storage unit I rent outside of town."

"I was going to ask about the car," he said. "Just not right now. So thanks for that. We'll talk about the storage unit."

"What else can I do for you?"

"We'd like you to come in for another chat."

"That's fine," said Jadeen. "I'll just be along for the ride."

The line was quiet for a moment.

"Counselor Knox, always a pleasure."

"You know that's not true," she said, "but thanks anyway."

"Would three this afternoon be convenient for you?" he asked.

I nodded.

"We'll be there," said Jadeen.

Before I left, she asked me to think hard about anything I might have forgotten to tell her, that might surprise her in the upcoming interview. I shook my head.

"Though I'd expect to be surprised," I said. "I don't think this guy is done laying traps. It's too big a part of the adventure."

"We got a major sicko here, don't we."

"Within my profession, the term sicko would not be considered an acceptable diagnosis."

"So what would you call him?"

"An asshole."

———— • ————

Detective Sergeant Noah Shapiro led us from the reception area, stopping for bottles of water along the way. Scrawny, with sloped shoulders and a sunken chest, he looked much younger than he really was. He wore cheap dress slacks and a striped polyester shirt. If it weren't for the holstered Glock on his hip, you might mistake him for a high school chemistry teacher.

He had a cramped private office off the squad room, windowless and unadorned, as if to make the privilege of privacy appear a little less privileged.

"Sit, sit," he said, after dragging an extra metal chair into the tiny room. "How're the kids, counselor?"

"Just like you folks," she said. "Nosy and unreliable."

He grinned at her.

"That's why you love us so much."

"Why aren't we in the interview room?" she asked.

"Cause it's just a chit-chat, like I told you."

"Okay, then," she said, "what do you have to say, since we're just chatting."

Shapiro took out a file and opened it on the desk.

"You know we have a nice relationship with the cyber security people at the FBI," he said.

"Only because it was revealed in open court," said Jadeen.

"Nevertheless, they discovered something interesting at ExciteAble Technologies." He looked at me. "You've been hacked."

"Is that good news or bad?" I asked.

"That depends. The hacker is the one who moved all that corporate money into your accounts. Wouldn't be you, would it?"

"Can't they trace it back?" asked Jadeen.

"They're trying, but it's tough going. The bad guys are getting really good at this stuff," said Shapiro. "Before a hacker arrives at your door, he could have traveled all around the world, jumping from computer to computer, and disguising his point of origin with every stop along the way. Even the NSA can be stymied in working back to the source."

"I know how to use Google, and send and receive e-mail," I said. "That's the extent of my computer expertise."

Jadeen asked Shapiro if he wasn't starting to feel that some crazy guy was actually trying to screw over her client.

"Something like that, just not in those exact terms."

"So every minute you spend on Dr. Waters is a minute away from catching the actual perpetrator," she said.

Shapiro took off his glasses and rubbed his face, hard enough to leave red splotches. He put the glasses back on before responding.

"Thank you for that observation, Ms. Knox. It's wonderful to have one's priorities clarified."

"You're welcome," she said.

He turned to me.

"People at your company," he said, "anyone smart enough to do this? Some IT creep?"

"We have IT people," I said. "Smart enough, probably. But no creeps. We screen for that. I screen for that. It's part of my job."

"Do you screen for potential violent behavior?"

"Not specifically. If I smell anything close to excessive aggression, they're gone."

"But you could have screwed up," said Shapiro.

"I could have. The guy in question would be uniquely skilled at hiding that part of his personality, and keeping it hidden. Does it by reflex."

"That sounds like a profile," said Shapiro.

"Just a guess, based on what little I know."

"Pettigrew says you know your stuff."

"So does he. He'll tell you none of this fits with my personality," I said.

"Really," said Shapiro. "So not skilled at making up crazy shit just to mess with people's heads?"

"Just cause a man can do something, doesn't mean he's doing it, Detective," said Jadeen, "and chit-chats don't include insinuations, however you dress 'em up."

"You're right," he said, slapping his hands down on his desk. "Sorry. It's a habit of mine. Because I'm, what, a homicide investigator?"

Shapiro used the rest of our time to arrange access to my car and storage unit. All the while, Jadeen pressed him for more information, but he cheerfully assured us that was all he had. She pretended to take him at his word.

I actually thought he was telling the truth, having reviewed his file with Pettigrew during a routine evaluation of New Haven's detective squads. Shapiro was probably the straightest arrow on the force, having only a scattering of abuse accusations, all easily dismissed based on concrete evidence. A grandson of Holocaust victims, the son of a suicidal mother, and a family man who rarely mentioned his family, the worst I could identify was a touch of paranoia, though justified by his background. What some like me would call a realistic pathology.

You might also wonder why a man with his IQ, pushing the genius range, would spend his life as a cop. I'd seen IQ scores of hundreds of cops, so it didn't surprise me a bit.

"I get it, Detective," I said, "but it's a dead end. Stop wasting time on me."

He took my hand and forced me to shake.

"More good advice," he said. "I will try to follow it."

Chapter Four

Before Shapiro had a chance to search my storage unit, the night supervisor for the storage company opened it up and found Paresh's body. A former cop, he recognized the odor seeping out the big door. One of my stored items was an antique chair, where the headless Paresh sat with his right hand held aloft by an artful use of pine splints and duct tape. The middle finger of the hand was where you'd expect it to be.

This time, when he called me in to discuss the developments, we were in Interview Room One, with two video cameras mounted overhead to capture both sides of the table. Jadeen sat next to me and Andy Pettigrew sat across the table with Noah Shapiro.

Neither man seemed much in the mood for small talk or breezy bonhomie.

Jadeen felt the same way, though she nearly always did.

"Dr. Waters voluntarily told you about the storage unit," she said, by way of kicking off the interview.

The men across the table took a while to respond, then Shapiro said, "Usually, that'd be lovely. But this kind of thing just keeps on happening. What's next, Dr. Waters?"

"I don't know," I said. "But it'll be something."

"Very helpful," said Shapiro.

"I think Waters believes the killer has a thing for the dramatic," said Pettigrew. "Surprise being an important feature. Would you agree?" he added, looking at me.

"Yes."

Shapiro sat back in his chair, and slumped down so far I thought he might slide off onto the floor.

"Do you know the odds of guessing a four-digit code?" he asked me.

"No," I said, "but pretty low."

"One in ten thousand. My statistics professor said that once your odds get that low, it might as well be zero."

"I sucked at statistics," I said. "Almost wrecked my master's degree, which would have killed the chance at a PhD."

"That storage unit had a special hardened, four-digit combination lock," said Shapiro. "Yet it was intact when the manager smashed off the hasp with a sledge hammer. So how did the killer get that body in there?"

"You got security cam recordings?" asked Jadeen.

"Somebody tampered with that particular camera," he said.

"Resourceful," I said. The other three turned their heads to me. "He's very resourceful. It's gamesmanship. Cover all the angles, think through all the contingencies. Exciting for anybody, but for people like this guy, it's nearly orgasmic."

Shapiro looked over at Pettigrew, who nodded his head.

"You like those kinds of games?" Shapiro asked me.

"Yes," I said, yielding one of Jadeen's wide-eyed glowers. A visual scream. "I've played in the Great Escape tournament for ten years. Developed by military special ops. Everyone gets dropped off at a location unknown to them, and we have to make it back to home base without being detected by dozens of pursuers." I looked at Jadeen. "It's public knowledge."

"They can bring along a backpack," said Pettigrew. "Contents up to them. That's the key—knowing what to bring and how to plan proper deployment."

Shapiro straightened himself in his chair.

"You must be one clever son of a bitch," he said.

"Not really. I do a lot of team building, creative thinking exercises at ExciteAble. I use the Great Escape competitions to hone those skills."

"That kind of thing makes me glad I sit home at night and watch TV," said Shapiro.

"Just means you'll have an earlier than necessary death," I told him. "But that's your choice."

There were no clocks in the interview room. And no pictures on the wall, or extra furniture. A sparseness so spare it actually sharpened my mental acuity, not the cops' intent.

"A team-building expert who never played sports," said Shapiro.

"Wrestling and weight lifting," I said. "Many consider those sports."

"But not team sports. Odd for an expert in team building. You must do a lot of research."

Jadeen had so much body language going on that Shapiro and I both looked at her.

"What the hell is all of this about?" she asked. "Do you want to know if he went to the high school dance? Relevance, Detective, or we're done here."

Shapiro really seemed to enjoy her, if his kind smile was any proof.

"We're not in court, Jadeen. I'm just curious about your client's general attitude about people. As in, he's a pretty self-contained guy. And yet his job is all about improving human interaction. You don't see any contradictions there?"

Jadeen took that moment to drill Pettigrew with her large dark eyes.

"Ask your pet shrink," she said. "He's been working with Dr. Waters for years. And don't deny it, this conversation's gettin' recorded. And I know how to get a subpoena."

Shapiro lost the urge to look up at the camera in the corner of the room. He sat way back in his chair again, gripping the edge of the table.

"Dr. Pettigrew?" he said.

Pettigrew took a professorial pause, then said, "Dr. Waters tends to introversion, but is not remotely antisocial. Just comfortable engaging in solitary pursuits. I'm the same way. I like you people fine, but on Saturdays, it's just me and my garden."

Shapiro pulled himself up from the slump and put both hands under his chin, leaning on the table.

"I get it, Waters," he said. "I really do. If it weren't for my family, I'd be the ultimate lonely guy."

"I'm not lonely. I just keep to myself. Mostly." I told him about Skinny McDowell's. "They can tell you I know how to form complete sentences and only rarely talk about chopping off people's heads."

This forced him back into the slump, as if drawn there involuntarily. I could see the debate on his face: get aggressive and try to gain dominance, or stick with empathy. He was a good interviewer, so empathy won.

"I don't know what the hell is going on here," said Jadeen. "But if I don't hear any charges, or substantive matters relating to this case, me and my client are seriously out of here."

The claustrophobic little room went silent, with no one letting their face give up their thoughts, though I could almost hear Shapiro's pleasure with Jadeen. I grinned at him, so he knew I knew.

"So get the hell out of here," he said to her. "But not too far," he said to me. "I'm thinking we'll have more to chat about, and I'd hate to have you traveling all the way back from who knows where."

I thanked him and let myself be dragged out of there by Jadeen, who'd made an impressive performance out of rising from her chair, packing up her briefcase, and stalking toward the door.

Once outside she said, "You talk too much, Waters. Next time we need to go through things in advance. Be better prepared."

I reached out my hand, which she reluctantly shook.

"I will. I know I'm in trouble," I said. "I hope you'll hang in there with me."

And then I walked away, leaving behind her scowl and internal war between the love of justice and a deep belief that most of her clientele usually got exactly what they deserved.

CHAPTER FIVE

A few days later I was in my hotel room when Megan Rajput called. I was surprised because I'd changed my cell number. Then I remembered sharing it with Andy Pettigrew. Who obviously shared it with her.

"I'm on your side," she said.

"That's good. Nice to hear it."

"I never once thought it was you. You have too good an aura. Sort of rough around the edges, but good."

"Thanks, I think."

"Come see me."

"I can't. The press is watching the company. They'll pounce."

"I'll have a guy smuggle you in. I've already lined him up."

I didn't add that the cops were probably watching my every move as well. Because I already knew how to handle that.

"Who's the guy?"

She told me. Carmine Fusco, a second-shift supervisor at the company who'd been with the Rajputs almost from the beginning.

"I'll take it from here," I told her.

When I got off the phone, I logged on to the company's help desk and grabbed Fusco's cell number. He was ready for me.

"Just give me your address and I'll come get you," he said.

Instead, I gave him the address of a parking garage where I told him to pick me up in an hour. I'd be on the third floor in front of the stairwell. If he was more than five minutes late, I'd be gone and we'd try something else.

The garage served an office building that had a bank branch on the first floor, accessible by the street and a small retail mall, which had its own inside parking. I drove to the mall and cut through the bank, timing my arrival at the other garage perfectly. Fusco swept up in a grey Chevy Suburban and I jumped inside.

"Hey, Dr. Waters," he said. "How ya doin'?"

"Doin' fine, Carmine, all things considered. And just plain Waters is okay with me."

He was big enough to fit the scale of the SUV. Thick around the middle and wearing a five o'clock shadow that probably sprouted before noon. A golf-ball sized class ring took up half of his left middle finger. Tobacco smell clung to the air, but the interior of the SUV was uncluttered and dust-free. A kid's car seat was in the back. He saw me look back at it.

"My granddaughter's," he said. "I got chauffeur duty in the mornings."

"Probably the safest ride in New Haven."

"That would undoubtedly be true," he said.

We rode the rest of the way in near silence. When we reached the company, he drove up to a side door next to the loading bays. He told me where to go from there and I made my exit. No thank-yous were necessary, though I thanked him anyway.

It was a simple walk down the hall and a right turn into an empty office. I remembered it once belonged to a shipping foreman I'd bounced the year before after he'd grabbed a dispatcher's rear end. We gave her his job and moved her into the regular office suite, though she still spent most of her time around the bays. There was no subsequent harassment.

The office was musty and festooned with abandoned relics of the ejected foreman. Softball trophies, a poster of Derek Jeter cracking a home run, an empty bottle of Jack Daniel's with a tiny bra tied around its neck.

Megan Rajput sat behind the desk.

"Nice to see you, Waters," she said, rising up to give me an awkward hug, and an even more awkward kiss that landed closer to my lips than my cheek. Her face looked a little pale under the freckles, and a gloss of sweat covered her forehead and upper lip. A touch of wine graced her breath.

I handed her a cashier's check for $260,000, which included the money deposited in my account and the amount that paid off my mortgage.

"You don't have to do this," she said. "I mean, not now."

"Thanks for that, Megan, but I really do."

She searched around for a pocket, and not finding any, tucked the check into her shirt.

"You look good," she said. "Me, I'm an entire wreck."

"Not so bad," I said, as we both sat down. "Considering what you're going through."

"You don't know the half of it. Correction. Basically none of it. Do you mind if I smoke?"

"You can do anything you want. It's your company."

She smirked while digging a pack of cigarettes out of her purse and lighting up.

"That's the theory. Though you'd never know it from the way people treat me here."

I waited while she searched for an ashtray, ultimately choosing a bottle cap from the trash, which quickly filled up, spilling the ashes onto the desk.

"What do you mean by that?" I asked her.

"They're still pretty freaked out, but the extra security and 24/7 counseling seems to be helping. Thanks again for that."

"So what's the issue?"

"It's nothing obvious," she said, with some reluctance. "Which is the point. Subtle resistance. Excessive politeness bordering on condescension."

"They want you to know you're not Paresh. Though they're probably unaware of their own behavior. Primal response."

"Spoken like a true shrink. I've got some primal responses of my own, buddy."

"What about Nelson?" I asked. "He can help."

I was referring to Nelson Sarnac, the chairman of the board. He'd run a lot of companies, and was equally known, and often feared, around ExciteAble.

She dipped her head.

"I should probably reach out, but he scares me," she said.

"I'll do it," I said. "He'll talk to me. And if he doesn't, you need another board chairman."

"I need you," she said, her head still hung over the desk.

I thought about what to say.

"I'm persona non grata around here. I don't think talking to me is a good idea. If I did, we wouldn't be hiding in the loading docks."

"These are my loading docks," she said, more loudly than she should have.

"I know they are."

She seemed to gather herself up again. I waited. She looked hard into my eyes.

"Let's say Paresh mentioned names of people in the company a thousand times. How many times did he mention you?" she asked.

"No idea."

"Five hundred. No, I'm lying. Eight hundred."

"We worked closely together."

"He loved you," she said, more accusation than compliment. "Not that way. Loved the way you thought."

"That's pretty funny, given how smart he was."

"Smart people don't always understand other people. You do," she said.

She grabbed a wad of her thick red hair and started raking it with her fingers. I thought she might be starting to cry, but her eyes stayed dry.

"What kind of cruel god would give a person this kind of hair?" she asked.

"Adversity builds character."

"Yeah, bullshit."

"Agreed. Bullshit."

She dropped the strand of hair as if it was on fire.

"I'll call Nelson and tell him I want to work with both of you as advisors. All on the q.t.," she said.

"Meeting could be tricky."

"We'll meet on the computer," she said. "I do it all the time with my niece. She's in college in California."

"Okay. What sort of advice are you looking for?" I asked her.

"What do you think? What am I going to do with this place?"

"Sell it."

She didn't like that.

"You don't think I'm capable of running it."

I regretted being so abrupt. And surprised myself, having spent so many years within those walls choosing my words with far more care.

"I think you're a very capable person. I'm sorry for implying otherwise. Let's step back and talk about what this thing is." I looked around the room as if to conjure an image of the company as a whole. "At the heart of every successful enterprise is a management group that reminds me of successful rock bands, or basketball teams. A small set of people, each with distinctive abilities who together express a unified whole. You can define each individual's role and graph out how they come together, perform as a team. You can even swap out some of the players and see improvement, but when you try to replicate that dynamic with all new people, it never works. And in my opinion, it's because inside every successful team is a hot core of leadership. It can be one person, two at the most, who define and drive a company's central nervous system. At ExciteAble, it was me and Paresh. I'm replaceable. He's not."

She sat quietly for a moment, though with her shoulders back and expression firm, if not exactly defiant.

"He wasn't the only genius in the sea," she said. "I know plenty of them."

I didn't know exactly what she meant by that. Which she could tell.

"You weren't around at the beginning," she said. "We were part of a crowd, a network of friends and others working on related technology. There was a lot of sharing, and a lot of late nights, and not much sobriety. Geek heaven. This tapered off as companies started to form and patents were getting written. But we all stayed in touch. Some of those guys are still good friends. They've all called."

This didn't completely surprise me. It made historic sense. I'd just never heard about this side of Rajput's life. I was so focused on the company at hand I never asked how it got there in the first place.

"That's good, Megan. Maybe you can reconstitute. I shouldn't have jumped to conclusions."

"Quit apologizing," she said, "and tell me you'll help."

"That's up to you, Megan. You're the one who'll face the blowback, if there is any. Though that'd be moot if they decide to charge me."

"You think that's possible?" she asked in a small voice.

"Yes. But not likely since I didn't do it."

I didn't see a reason to give further details. And from what I could read on her face, I hadn't degraded my standing. She looked more distressed for me than for herself.

"We'll burn that bridge when we come to it," she said, with a weak grin.

Since I already had a driver, I took the opportunity to go directly to Nelson Sarnac's house in Old Lyme, a coastal village a half hour east of New Haven. Megan cleared the way with a phone call while I was still with her in the shipping department. Only hearing her side of the conversation, I didn't know what kind of reception I'd get, but at least he agreed to the meeting.

The house was a location scout's vision of a classic New England colonial—a barn red, two-story saltbox with a center chimney, set like a precious relic on a cushion of luxuriant summertime foliage. A weather-beaten Mercedes station wagon was in the gravel driveway and a brace of golden labs, one considerably older than the other, formed the greeting committee.

Sarnac met me at the front door—a short, round guy reeking of cigar smoke and disdain for the conventions of good health. At seventy-two, undiminished in mind and vitality, he could make a case for his lifestyle choices.

"Waters," he said, waving me into the house. "Good thing you caught me when you did. I was about to run the dogs down to the pond."

"We can still do that."

I didn't know much about his past, beyond his success with a string of manufacturing outfits that made equipment for Electric Boat, the submarine builders headquartered another half hour down the coast. He'd sold all his companies after his wife died but kept busy captaining the boards of several local firms, notably ExciteAble Technologies. My interaction had amounted to a few board presentations, and one celebration of the firm's twelfth anniversary, where we had a conversation focused entirely on ExciteAble, devoid of all small talk or humor whatsoever.

Before we left the house, he pulled on a pair of muddy L.L. Bean hunting boots, only glancing once at my running shoes. Though as it turned out, the path through the backyard and small stand of hemlock and maple was reasonably dry. The dogs led the way ahead of Sarnac, who had a lit cigar in his hand, with me bringing up the rear, wading through the noxious vapors.

When we got to the pond, the dogs sat and stared at him, trembling with anticipation. He tossed a pair of tennis balls into the water, and they were off.

"Paresh," he said. "Hell of a thing."

"I had nothing to do with it," I said.

"Of course you didn't. Unless you did, but that's not what we're here to talk about."

"Good."

"Mrs. Rajput thinks you'd be of some value as an advisor."

"She said the same about you."

He gave the type of little laugh that some might interpret as a scoff.

"I guess so, since it's what I do."

"I don't know much about operations," I said. "My deal is the people. How they think and act."

"In other words, how big a pain in the ass," he said.

"Sometimes."

The dogs came back to shore and galloped up to Sarnac, dropping the balls at his feet before shaking out their fur, which sent plumes of spray into the air, causing him to take a step back.

He yelled out a string of commands, on which they walked back to the pond and repeated the action, resulting in far less water filling the air.

"Knuckleheads," he said, tossing the balls back in the water. "So what does Megan really want?" he asked.

"What she told you. Advice. She wants us to work together."

"And what does that mean?"

"I don't know. You're the chairman of the board, and a capable businessman. I was Paresh's principal advisor. She might think our combined abilities would have some value for the firm."

"And what do you think?"

"I serve at Mrs. Rajput's pleasure. If she wants to give it a try, so do I."

"Where did you work before coming to ExciteAble?" he asked, using the butt end of his cigar as a pointer.

"I worked for myself."

"Doing what?"

"Playing poker. That's where I met Paresh. He was a regular Saturday night at the casino. Excellent player."

"Why'd you leave?" he asked.

"You know why."

He tried to look surprised.

"What do you mean?"

"You're funneling me into this line of conversation. You did a background check and learned I'd been blackballed from the casino. You should also know they reversed the decision." He just looked at me, trying to keep his face set at neutral, unaware of the triumphalism written across his imperious mouth and jutting jaw.

"So you're a cheat."

"No, I'm just better than most at spotting tells. It's why the casino hired me, to actually catch cheaters. You know that too."

"And Paresh hired you away," said Sarnac.

"He did."

"Why?"

"Because I could always tell if he had a good hand or not," I said.

"So you cheated him too."

"No. I helped him."

"Why would you do that?"

"Because I liked him. He was a good man."

He took an unfortunately big drag off the cigar and sent the resulting smoke my way. I fought the cough.

"Okay. Maybe we could work together," he said.

"No way," I told him, and started back up the path.

"Waters," he called after me.

I stopped.

"What?"

"Come on back here."

"Why?"

"I want to have a discussion."

"I don't see any point in that."

The dogs flew out of the water, stopped well short of Sarnac, and shook out their fur. Then they ran the rest of the way, dropping the balls at his feet. They sat again, waiting for round three.

"Working with me could be very good for you," Sarnac said.

I walked back to him, reached down, and picked up the balls. The dogs leapt to their feet and leaned toward the pond, their eyes fixed unblinking on the balls. My toss went all the way to the opposite shore, the balls bouncing into the woods.

"I don't submit to asymmetrical relationships," I told him.

A little pink formed beneath his glassy, old man's skin.

"I just said we can team up."

"You did. In a tone that foreshadows a style of persistent domination. It's what you're used to, I understand. But it doesn't work for me."

He pointed at me again, this time with the lit end of the cigar.

"This is about compensation, isn't it?" he said.

"You would say that, too, because that's how you think. I'm still drawing my salary, and for the time being, that's compensation enough."

Then I left again, and he didn't call me back. I heard the dogs emerge from the pond, a frantic rustle of sodden skin and fur, which in my mind's eye I hoped was an atomized shower on the way to saturating Sarnac's country gentleman's clothes.

CHAPTER SIX

I made it to the gym the next morning, elated to be back after a few days away from the dank, sweaty, overlit weight room. I did extra floor stretches to avoid possible injury and started with an undemanding routine.

It was early, so only one other lifter was in the room, a young woman with a deep natural tan and a near grimace of concentration. In accordance with weight room customs, she acted as if I wasn't there, saying nothing to me, and I said nothing to her.

I ramped up carefully, and an hour later I was back in full form, hoisting maximum workout weights and sparing little. For some, this was the cathartic, spiritual experience of a good workout. For me, it was an effective dopamine transmission and a salubrious release of endorphins.

Either way, I felt a lot better for it.

I looked at my phone after taking a shower and saw a text message from Olivia Lefèvre. The ID on the phone was actually Sinclair Importing, the name I'd chosen for her as an amateurish layer of security.

It said, "Give me a buzz."

I used the number for what she called her "deep, double-undercover communications device."

"I've been reading about you," she said. "Things are getting interesting."

We'd last spoken immediately after Paresh's murder, when I filled her in as well as I could and assured her I was fine and would remain so. I hadn't talked to her since then, but that was part of the deal. She called, I answered. Never the other way around.

"You think?"

"I think it's time to review the contract," she said.

"Overdue. What are the new terms?"

"Twelve point twenty-two," she said.

"Okay. Look forward to the negotiation."

"Indeed."

I'd met her the year before at a conference of human resource professionals, arguably the least scorching, libidinous venue you can find. I was there to hold a workshop on employee motivation and she was there to escape for a few days from her high-stress job as an executive recruiter. We sat in a circle, like an encounter group, which is more or less what the workshop became, as the participants drifted into discussing their deepest frustrations and failures of confidence. Olivia did none of that, nor did I, though she did spend the session frowning at me with a mixture of antagonism and curiosity.

Later, I saw her at the hotel bar, where she was nursing a Scotch on the rocks and radiating subterranean signals to the guys in the bar to stay clear. I sat next to her and asked if she was satisfied with her résumé.

"I am," she said.

"Then why haven't you sent it out yet?"

"I don't know. Do you think it's the Stockholm Syndrome? Am I infatuated with my captors?"

"More likely you're not sure you want to stay in your profession."

"I love my profession," she said. "What do you want to drink?"

"What you're drinking. So later you can't claim I had an unfair advantage."

"Later?"

"Tomorrow morning."

The evening took the predictable course, if you lucked into the proper prediction, which I did. And it wasn't until the next morning that I learned she was a married woman.

"He's a PI," she said. "Former homicide detective with the NYPD. His name is Erik. With a K."

"And a good guy."

"Sort of."

"And you love him."

"Very much," she said.

"But he doesn't entirely trust you."

"No. And stop doing that."

"What?"

"Reading my mind."

"Sorry," I said. "Occupational hazard."

"I can read yours too. You're wondering why I'm naked in bed with you with my head resting on your shoulder."

"Because it's more comfortable than standing on your head?"

"He's programmed to protect. Me above all others. Which means it gets a little smothering. Why do men think they can control you and still maintain their own distance whenever they feel like it?"

"Why do women let them?" I said.

"Are you always this candid?"

I admitted I wasn't. That sometimes I spun the truth if it served a greater good. Though this wasn't one of those times. She accepted that, and we had another round, and spent the next day and night together, and since then had maintained a fierce, albeit episodic, relationship.

Olivia had many fine qualities, and others you might not categorize as particularly fine. At the forefront was a highly refined paranoia. Maybe this should have been obvious, given that she was cheating on a man uniquely capable of uncovering her infidelity. Though I always felt she took to the challenge with a dash of brio. An eagerness to prove her cleverness and intellectual superiority.

For my part, I really liked this woman. I'd say I loved her, if I was confident in the word love, which for me had too evanescent a quality to fully embrace. I just knew I felt at home with her. We never argued, never disappointed each other, never hurt each other's feelings. Our time together, restricted as it was, was lived on an elevated plane of good humor and mutual regard. Of calm, entertaining conversations, and pleasant periods of serene silence.

Our coded phone conversation that day was for us to meet at a particular country hotel, miles from New Haven, on a specific date and time. It was easy for me. I just went there and waited at the bar. For her, it was a day of convoluted travel, double-reverse maneuvers, disguises, and heightened awareness. Tradecraft that would honor the most experienced secret agent.

As a consequence, she always arrived, silent as a stalker, to the barstool next to me, slightly flushed and breathing heavily through her nose.

"I'll take one of those," she said, pointing to my Scotch.

The bartender was already on the way.

"How're we doing?" I asked.

"Better now. You look pretty good for a murder suspect. Though I'm not exactly sure how they're supposed to look."

"Confident. Outraged. Or put upon. Or guilty as hell. I've seen all four."

"And who's actually guilty?" she asked.

"I don't know, but it wasn't me. You might not call me a people person, but I draw the line at killing them."

"And they're letting you run free if you're the suspect?" she asked. "Sure you weren't followed?"

"They can't restrain me unless I'm actually charged. And no police force in the country can afford to follow their suspects around."

"That's a relief."

I took the next hour or so bringing her up to speed. I tried to be clear and she listened carefully, a skill she'd learned interviewing masters of the universe. Listening and remembering everything that was spoken.

"You pissed off somebody," she said, when I finished.

"I've heard that before."

"You won't mind if we don't visit your storage unit again," she said, referring to one of our occasional meeting places. Much less luxurious than a hotel room, though decidedly more secure.

"As soon as the cops let me, everything goes to the dump and a cleaning crew goes in there with a few gallons of bleach."

"So sorry," she said. "That was an exciting place. Cold, dark, and nasty."

We got another round of drinks and I took that moment to say that she was beautiful and desirable, and to lean in just a little closer so I could kiss her on the cheek.

She did as I asked, while noting this would be a good time for her husband, Erik, to put a bullet through my temple with his sound-suppressed .44 semiautomatic. If he happened to be lurking nearby.

"My goal," I said, "is to die happy and fast. In that order."

After I kissed her, she looked around the bar.

"I guess he's not out there. So much for your short, happy life."

"You really do look great," I said.

"Abstinence makes the heart grow fonder."

"How do you know I've been abstaining?"

Olivia was a lovely woman, to me, partly because I liked parts of her that others might see as flaws. Like her crooked grin, caused by a childhood nerve disorder, and her unfussed-over coarse blonde hair. Cheekbones that were maybe a little too sharp and hands that belonged on a dairy farmer. I shared these thoughts with her, as we sat on the barstools, and she contended that romantic attraction was a hallucinatory drug, but so what. Without it, human beings wouldn't be overrunning the planet.

"Anyway, you actually love me for what's inside my skull," she said, "right?"

"I do."

And I did. After years of experimenting with incompatible personalities, I'd discovered the wonders of like-mindedness. The only hitch was it came encumbered by a possessive, controlling husband with a gun. And a reluctance on her part to unload that burden, for reasons that were opaque to me, like-mindedness aside. But I never pressed her, or even questioned the arrangement, for fear it would break the spell, and shatter any possibility for the future.

That may sound irrational. It's irrational to me, but that's what I did.

It wasn't until later that night, when we were sitting in opposite overstuffed chairs wrapped in bedding that I asked her if she really thought Erik would shoot me in the head if he caught us kissing.

She gave it some thought, then admitted she wasn't sure.

"I don't really know how his mind works. I live with a particular version of Erik, who is a reasonable, generous, and even occasionally tender man. But there are other Eriks in there who are entirely inaccessible. Have you ever heard of that, Captain Psychologist?"

"I've never met him, so I can't have an opinion on his individual state of mind. I know most people compartmentalize, some to a very refined degree. Typical of cops, soldiers, dictators, even criminals, who need a hard wall between their jobs and the family at home. Some can sustain it, others not so well."

Olivia came over and squeezed herself into my chair. I told her we were paying good money for that hotel room, which had plenty of furniture for everybody.

"I want you to meet him sometime," she said. "So you can have an opinion."

"I'll do whatever you want, but not a great idea."

"He'll figure it out?"

"Not from me."

"Should I be insulted by that?"

"If you want. Like I said, I never met the guy, so I don't know how good he is at reading the situation. In fact, given what's been happening to me, I'm a little worried, for both of us."

She burrowed deeper in the chair, exhausting all the remaining space.

"Okay, buzz kill. Let's schmoosh around a little, then get room service on the phone. There's got to be more Scotch down there."

She left soon after that and I stayed till the next morning, sleeping off and on, and thinking, despite myself, about Erik with a K. Up until then, I'd willfully imagined him as a fantastical figure, Olivia's preoccupation, but immaterial to me. I realized, lying on the sweaty sheets in the luxuriant hotel room, that it was a rationalization I could no longer afford.

That day I called Megan Rajput and asked who at Excite-Able had direct control over IT, in particular, the accounting software. She said that would have to be our CFO, Colin Brice.

"How's he taking it?" I asked.

"Didn't quit, so I guess he's taking it well enough. He's busy, that I know. A good man."

He'd been with ExciteAble for less than a year, an emergency hire after his predecessor left us in the wake of personal and professional fiascoes. We were rightly concerned that we get it right after that, and apparently we had.

"I need to talk to him."

"Okay, but you still shouldn't come into the office. It doesn't sound like your chat with Nelson went so well."

"I was wrong to think he's your friend," I said. "I'd keep him on the board, but at arm's length."

She pressed me on how I came to that conclusion, but there was no easy way to explain it over the phone. So I was honest and told her I needed time to answer properly. She took that well enough and went back to Brice, whom Megan said would be contacting me as soon as she got to him. I thanked her and rang off.

The next thing I did was have a conversation with myself. I needed to settle on some common-sense assumptions if

I was going to operate in the world. As I told Olivia, the cops weren't following me around. I knew enough about police work to know surveillance was very expensive, and rarely employed on a long-term basis. Wiretapping, on the other hand, was relatively cheap and easy to do. It was also unlikely people were sitting around listening to recorded conversations. Rather, they could run recordings, then transcribe everything into searchable documents in case they had something specific to search for. So my smartphone had to be considered insecure.

The solution to that was pretty simple. I went to the closest big box store and bought a burner—a disposable, prepaid cell phone. Why this was still possible, given their popularity with the criminal class, was surprising, but I was glad for it. When Brice called me, I told him I'd call him back, which I did on my burner, using *69 to block the number as an extra precaution.

This also solved the problem of the mechanized voice calling and messing up my concentration.

I gave Brice the name of a pizza joint in a town just north of New Haven that had a bar in the back. He knew the place and agreed to meet me right after work.

As with most of the professional people I knew, I'd somewhat unconsciously established my own relationship with technology. Deciding I didn't have the time, mental space or inclination to become expert, I learned what I needed to learn to be functional and disregarded the rest. I had no reason to regret this until the moment I realized how ill prepared I was to talk tech with Colin Brice.

If the stresses of the last few weeks had gotten to him, it didn't show. His handshake was as eager and firm as the last time we shook. Even in the dim light of the bar he looked bright-eyed, his youthful vigor reinforced by a full head of soft brown hair, always a little past time for a haircut. He was drinking an imported beer. I ordered the same.

I thanked him for meeting me.

"Megan asks, I do," he said.

"Did she tell you I wanted to keep it confidential?"

"Sure. As long as it's legal, ethical, and moral, I'm good."

"Fair enough."

I told him Detective Shapiro had revealed that Excite-Able's accounting system had been penetrated and manipulated to direct funds into my accounts. I was curious how that could have happened, and how the FBI found out about it.

"That's easy. I told them. Before I realized it was an inside job."

He started to explain the technology behind this discovery, but I told him to keep it on a layman's level.

"Pretend I'm a small child, or your grandmother," I said.

"Bad guy stuff, a virus, can infiltrate your computer and hide deep down in the core of the system. So deep you wouldn't necessarily know it was there until it started doing mischief. Fortunately, there are good guy programs that spot the mischief right away and just go in and zap the bug right out of there. That's what happened here. I got an alert."

The only task the bad guy software achieved was to transfer corporate funds into my account. The transaction was fairly simple, and the path easily followed. Brice just cleared out the virus and plugged the hole.

"Do you know how it got in there?" I asked.

"Can never know 100 percent, but I think through the front door. So technically, not a hack."

"Meaning?"

"The administrative password. Somebody just sat down at a secure computer, opened the accounting system, typed in the password, and went to work. He could have just made the transactions and it would have gone unnoticed until the audit, or some other standard procedure turned it up. But he installed this little subprogram that allowed for ongoing mischief."

I asked if that meant we were dealing with a sophisticated computer whiz. He said, sadly, no.

"I could write the code in about two hours, give it to you on a flash drive, with step-by-step instructions, and you could do the install in the time it takes to make a pot of coffee. If you had the password."

"Who at the company had the password?"

"Five people in accounting, IT manager Bonnie Cardoni, and me. And Paresh, of course. Though he never went near accounting. That's what I'm for."

"Is there any way to trace it back?"

Shapiro had told me that tracking down bad actors who come in through the Internet was getting tougher and tougher, even for federal cyber warriors. But Brice said that was irrelevant in this case.

"Why?" I asked.

"Because the virus was installed between midnight and five A.M. when the accounting system isn't plugged into the Internet. So it was impossible to hack in. The logs are clear on that. Like I said, technically not a hack."

"So why tell the FBI?"

He smiled an indulgent smile.

"This stuff is complicated. My fiduciary responsibility to the firm is trumped by legal responsibilities, which could affect my CPA. I dropped the dime as soon as I discovered the financial funny business. It was only later that I determined the funny business was all internal. You not only have to have the password, but you can only access the accounting system from designated computers. You were my first choice, but you never went near the folders in question. Otherwise, we wouldn't be having this conversation. The other accounting people also checked out."

"So whose computer was used to make the transfers into my account?" I asked.

He didn't have to say it, since I could read it on his face.

"Paresh Rajput's," I said, and he nodded.

CHAPTER SEVEN

When I got back to my hotel room and flicked on the light switch, nothing happened. I flicked it a few more times with no result. I had a tiny flashlight on my key ring, which I used to shoot a narrow beam into the room. Nothing looked out of place, though there was too little light to know for sure. I walked into the bathroom and flicked the switch, but that light was also out. Though the fan worked.

I shot the beam up at the ceiling and saw that the light fixture had been opened and the bulb removed. I took a step into the main part of the room and scanned again with the little flashlight, which is when I saw a plain cardboard box sitting on the floor at the foot of the bed. A nearly invisible string ran from the box to a leg of the desk and bureau combo. I edged back out of the room, closed the door, and called Detective Shapiro.

I told him the situation. Minutes later hotel security was clearing out the rooms, beginning with my terrified neighbors, and in the midst of that, the New Haven PD bomb squad showed up in full regalia. Detective Shapiro appeared soon after. We strayed outside to give the CSIs some elbow room. He had me describe everything in detail.

"How long were you gone from the room?" he asked.

I told him maybe two hours at most. He asked to see my car. We went over there and he put on a pair of surgical gloves, then pulled out a thin, plastic flashlight with a brilliant LED beam. He wiggled under the rear of the car and I could see the light moving around the chassis. He came back out again and walked around to the left rear of the car, where he crouched down and reached into the wheel well. When he stood up again he held a small black device.

"GPS tracker," he said.

It would tell the killer that I'd left the hotel and driven far enough away to give him time to get into my room, place the box, pull all the lightbulbs, and get out.

We didn't know how he got a key. Or how long he'd been tracking my movements. Carmine Fusco had driven me to ExciteAble when I visited Megan, and subsequently Nelson Sarnac. But when I met Olivia Lefèvre for an overnight, I was in my own car.

As if hearing these thoughts, Shapiro said the device looked fresh and clean. His guess was it hadn't been in the wheel well all that long.

"We've had a lot of weather in the last few weeks. It would show," he said. "Though that's just speculation. I'll trace the purchase and check for prints and DNA, but don't expect anything."

"You still think I'm faking all this?" I said.

"I'd tell you no, but we're allowed to lie to our suspects, so you wouldn't believe me anyway."

"I might. Let's see what the bomb squad comes up with."

I had till late the next day to find out, since they took the box to a remote location where they dealt with that kind of thing. Yet again, I had to get another room and leave all my stuff behind in what was another crime scene. There were plenty of rooms to choose from since most of the guests had beat the hell out of there.

The next morning Shapiro called to say the box was full of explosives. Only no more powerful than what a bunch of kids would set off on the Fourth of July.

Firecrackers.

"The head of the bomb squad said, 'The intent here was to terrify the victim, not cause any greater bodily injury than numb ears and screwed-up nerves.' So how're the nerves?"

"Fine," I said, "I predicted something like that. He's not done with me yet. I just wasn't sure, and others could have been hurt."

"You actually do care about people, don't you, Waters."

"Especially innocent people. Even psycho killers have their soft spots."

"Is that an official statement?"

"No, just a few words made in jest," I said.

As if sensing through the ether that I was making reckless declarations, my next call came in from my lawyer, Jadeen Knox.

"Pretty soon we're gonna be petitioning for protective custody," she said.

"Protecting me from myself?"

"Time for me to have a little sit-down with that detective."

Later that day a patrol cop showed up with all my stuff from the crime scene. Aside from being crammed in two big plastic bags, and covered with fingerprint dust, it was all in pretty good shape. I thanked her.

I checked out of the hotel, and after going over my car for fresh trackers, drove to the airport above Hartford and left it in a long-term parking lot. I stuffed a few essentials in a backpack and grabbed a cab to a Harley-Davidson dealership where I bought a four-year-old, blacked-out Harley 900 Sportster with two thousand miles on the odometer.

I was a little rusty at first, but it wasn't long before the ballet of steering, shifting gears, and easing the reliable Sportster around turns came back to me.

I avoided the four-lane highway on the way back toward New Haven to get used to the motorcycle before I had to share the road with tractor trailers and aggressive New England drivers, for whom posted speed limits were merely advisory.

I got as far as the inner suburbs, where I went to a motel that Olivia and I had made use of a few times, that operated on the honor system regarding IDs for its cash-paying customers.

I registered as Jim Bronson and chose the far end of the motel where it was quieter and less likely that someone would see me roll the motorcycle into the room. One of the essentials I'd brought along was my laptop. The motel had a strong Wi-Fi connection, a necessity for its criminal clientele, which I used to access online banking so I could transfer various savings and money market funds into my checking account.

I texted a coded message to Olivia, telling her to use the burner's number. I used the same phone to order a pizza, which was delivered by the most nervous pizza delivery guy in Greater New Haven. I gave him a substantial tip and a friendly fist bump.

After eating, I maneuvered the motorcycle against the door and went to bed fully dressed with the lights on. As I lay there on my back, I listened to the various segments of the Waters brain argue over the necessity for all this, until my brother, the highest level of executive function, stepped in and told the rest of the gang that the man really needed to get a good night's sleep. So shut up and let him do it.

And I did.

The next morning over ham, wheat toast, and scrambled eggs, I went back to the profile I'd started to work up soon after Paresh was murdered. I jotted down the original list of traits:

> *Male.*
> *Narcissistic.*
> *Delusional.*
> *Capable of carrying out extreme acts of violence.*
> *Intelligent.*
> *Resourceful.*
> *A deep planner.*
> *Bold.*

And now I had a few more:

> *Purposeful.*
> *Cool headed.*
> *Technically adept.*
> *Sadistic.*

I looked at the entries critically. I decided that the one at the top, "male," was based more on statistical probability than empirical evidence, but left it there anyway. I also questioned "delusional," since that left out the possibility that he actually had rational, however misplaced, grievances. I crossed it out.

With that deletion, I was left with a description of someone who could be considered entirely sane, depending on the situation. Even with the dose of sadism. The clinical consensus was you could be cruel without being nuts.

All in all, a depressingly formidable set of attributes.

I'd chosen to study psychology, at the strong suggestion of my brother, who thought it the ideal path for a person who worked so hard to understand the human mind. One of his first lessons was that emotions were just a different form of thought, usually more powerful diviners of the truth, though far more difficult to interpret, buried as they were down there in the subconscious. The same thing they taught me in grad school.

So I sat there with my breakfast and struggled with the question, how did I really *feel* about what was going on?

The answer took a little time to emerge, but it finally did.

I was seriously, and nearly uncontrollably, pissed off.

I had a second storage unit I hadn't revealed to the cops, or Jadeen, or anyone else. It was in a far older version of rented storage than the garage-style units everyone knows. This was an old-fashioned warehouse in a decrepit industrial slum in Bridgeport, with units demarcated by wire cages and walls of banged-up lockers.

In one of those lockers I kept the most potent, pint-sized semiautomatic handgun in the world. Handmade in a place they refused to reveal, it cost about the same as a used car, weighed less than my wallet and could compete with a target rifle in distance and impact.

It was equipped with a plastic holster that slipped invisibly into the small of my back. I was uncertified, and the gun unregistered, and thus entirely illegal. But also untraceable, since I bought it with cash from a source who could care less about bureaucratic niceties.

It was the third iteration of a practice I'd started while still in college, when I was living in a house owned by one of my professors who was in Europe on sabbatical. It was a great deal for both of us. Free housing for me, and a reliable, socially isolated, compulsively tidy house sitter for him.

The house was in Arlington, an old suburb of Boston, with a mix of professionals, working people, and poor, and a big neighborhood of giant Victorians, including the professor's. I had the pick of bedrooms, but I liked the servant's quarters on the upper floor for the view and spare, sturdy appointments.

That was where I was sleeping the night two guys broke in through a basement window and were halfway through stripping out the TVs and stereo equipment and filling bags with the professor's silver and other valuables before I woke up. I ran naked into the hallway and yelled down the stairs. The sounds below paused for a moment, then I heard footsteps heading up toward me. I ran back into the room and slammed the door, unhappy to see there wasn't a lock. There was a landline, which I picked up, but there was no dial tone. I was the only college kid I knew who didn't have a cell phone, something I instantly regretted.

As the footsteps kept coming, I dragged a chest of drawers in front of the door and got into my pants just as they were trying to break through. I sat on the floor and shoved my back against the chest, getting only tentative purchase on a woven rug with my bare feet. The blows to the door radiated through the furniture and drove me forward about an inch at a time, distance I made up with an all-out effort that was just enough to click the latch closed again.

I heard agitated voices, as an argument commenced, but not exact words.

Then I heard a series of booms and felt the vibrations from large-caliber rounds going through the door over my head. I scurried on all fours over to the bed and wriggled down between the edge of the mattress and the wall. More shots were fired, and more angry words exchanged, until what I assumed was the wiser of the two burglars convincing the shooter to knock it off so they could get the hell out of there.

I waited for about a half hour to leave my spot between the bed and wall, get dressed, move the chest of drawers out of the way, and go downstairs. I went to the basement and spliced the phone wires back together, then went up to the kitchen and called the police.

The dispatcher had me stay on the line and gave me a blow-by-blow on the approach of the patrol cars, and subsequently, cops on foot. She said not to move and just wait for them to come through the open kitchen door. That was fine with me. She had a calm, friendly voice, and it was nice to have someone to chat with at that moment.

The next day, I went deep into a Southie neighborhood and bought a heavy black Colt .45 semiautomatic with the serial numbers filed off. I slept with that gun, when I could fall asleep, for the next five years. Only stowing it in the bedside table when I had company, thinking her finding a gun under my pillow might spoil the mood.

I replaced it with an illicit Glock after that, which made its way to the storage locker as time passed and the night terrors receded. By the time I moved into the apartment that became my condo, the Glock had given way to the little high-tech marvel that was now nestled against my back.

I was increasingly aware of the perils of not just possessing, but carrying, an illegal firearm, which until then I'd kept hidden in the locker. But the cherry bombs had finally peeled away the years of lessening vigilance, until I was back there in that big old house, naked, terrified, and inescapably vulnerable, promising myself I would never be in that situation again.

CHAPTER EIGHT

I heard that I was no longer an active suspect in the murder of Paresh Rajput from Jadeen Knox. It came by way of a text to my burner phone, which along with my laptop, I'd turned off for about twenty-four hours.

I was at the gym, where after a full-on workout, steam bath, and shower, I'd capitulated and pushed the on button.

I sent a message back, thanking her. Then I sent a text to Megan Rajput to share the news. She returned the message a few seconds later.

"Come on in," said the last sentence of the text. "We need you back at work."

Rather than go to the motel, I bought fresh clothes and drove to the nearest train station. I parked the Harley, went into New Haven, and took a cab from there to the office.

There was no welcoming committee, but neither were there stares or averted eyes. Just a few hellos and the occasional "Glad to have you back."

Joey Adams was slightly more demonstrative, his cheerful, bearded face lit with a full smile. We sat down in my office, as we often did in the morning, and reviewed the upcoming schedule. Half of it was filled with meetings with Megan, Colin Brice, and our chief engineer. Joey gave me a single sheet listing all the work in progress I'd left behind. I asked him about the current mood of the place.

"A frothy admixture of anger, paranoia, hopelessness, and naked ambition," he said, without hesitation.

"You practiced that."

"I did. We've lost a lot of employees, replacing maybe half of them so far. HR tells me recruiting is tough when questions drift toward how our main guy departed the company. People are taking long lunches and the parking lot is cleared out by five. And the work hasn't abated, so deadlines are slipping. Megan almost never leaves her office and the engineering staff has forgotten all those lessons you gave about making eye contact and expressing pleasantries. Cats are lying down with dogs and there's a bad moon on the right."

I asked him if that was about it.

"Aye, chief. Situation normal, all fucked up. My résumé is on the street, but I'll retrieve it if you think you'll be sticking around for a while."

I told him I'd try, and we triaged the backlog of work, beginning with the worst breakdowns in interdepartmental communications. After the insanity of recent times, it was gratifying to be back on the job, a familiar world with at least a framework of equipoise and familiarity. I'd almost forgotten such a place could exist.

Soon after Joey left, my office phone rang. Unknown number. I picked it up.

"So glad you're back," said the mechanical voice. "Everyone missed you. Oh, wait, no they didn't. They hate you. Let's make the next leave of absence a permanent solution, what do you say?"

On the way to see Megan, I walked by Bonnie Cardoni's office, where she was sitting, a rare occurrence for a person who was usually in the server room with her head buried in a jumble of electronic components, or flitting like a bumblebee from one minor crisis to another.

She looked up at me, stress filling her angular, young face, and said, "I'm sorry, I'll do it now."

"Do what?"

"Turn on your network access. They had me shut it off when you took your leave of absence. I just found out you're back and haven't gotten to it yet."

I said I fully understood, and that I'd only stopped by to ask a few questions. I walked in the office and closed the door behind me, which was a little disturbing to her, since I never had closed-door meetings with female employees. Especially when they were barely thirty and noticeably well-configured.

Luckily, she understood the shut door after we spent the next half hour talking about passwords and the accounting system. I had more questions, but she promised to see me again after I was done with Megan. As I stood to leave, she added one more thought.

"I change it every month, you know that, right?" she said.

"I didn't."

"The new one is given out at the first Monday financial meeting. I hand it to everyone on a little piece of paper, and tell them after they log in, to eat it. I say it's a joke every time, but some of those people still think I'm serious."

She used two hands to grip at her unkempt black hair.

"How many are in the meeting?"

"Five from accounting, Colin and me. Paresh used to come, so assume Megan will, too, now that she has Paresh's job and all his financial access privileges."

"You told me the password lets you into the house, but not everyone gets to go in all the rooms."

"Shit, yeah. The accounting drones only get into rooms they need to do their work," she said. "Very restricted."

"Who would be able to transfer large sums from the corporation into an employee's account?"

"The CEO, theoretically, but Paresh didn't know how to do things in the system. Which leaves the CFO and me, because we can do everything. Oh, and God. He also can do everything."

She stood up and noticed that her flannel shirt was only half-tucked into her painted-on leggings. I averted my eyes while she fixed things up. When I looked back she was checking her smartphone. "I don't mind talking about this," she said, "but I think you're late."

I thanked her, though I still had one more question.

"Is it possible to have the accounting system make a transaction, but not have it go through right away?" I asked her.

"Sure. You can put it in the system today and schedule it to execute next week, or next month. If you change your mind, you can go in there and manually reverse it out. As long as you get there in time."

"How far out can you schedule a transaction?"

"All the way to the end of the fiscal year. After that, you'd have to back date it, though our auditors have a term for that."

"What?"

"A serious no-no."

Our chief engineer was Fred Warner III, and I knew from his file that his father and grandfather were also engineers, and that his son was studying at Caltech. I imagined engineering Fred Warners stretching out into the infinite future.

He was also the tallest man in the company, at nearly six and a half feet. His handshake was less a grip than a soft, enveloping embrace. He said he was glad to have me back, and I believed him, since neither untruthfulness nor irony were part of his composition.

Megan and Colin were equally welcoming and we quickly got down to a grinding two-hour review and planning meeting. Fred's steady if doleful style was quite familiar to me, but this was my first full exposure to Megan and Colin in a business environment, and I was struck by both. Megan ran the meeting with little of her usual disorderly bemusement and Colin was a wellspring of enthusiasm and goodwill. More importantly, freewheeling and imaginative in ways I'd rarely seen in a financial person.

A few times I caught Megan's eye and her look said, "I told you so," even though she hadn't.

I had a chance to pretend she had when I stayed behind after the meeting.

"You said months ago that he was good," I told her. "You're right."

"I often am."

"You are, but I still have some advice."

"Naturally."

"Spend a lot more time walking around the halls and plant floor, making eye contact and asking people how they're doing. No frowning. Just happy face."

"Do you know how freaking busy I am?" she asked.

"Do what I suggest and you'll be less busy, or at least you can spend more time on things that matter."

"Did Paresh do everything you suggested?"

"No. Though mostly. I only suggested things we both knew would work."

"You were a great team," she said, and without warning began to tear up.

"That's another thing," I said.

"What."

"Never let anyone see you cry, which you do a lot. It's especially bad for female CEOs. It's not fair, but that's the way it is."

"I guess I shouldn't confuse people smarts with sensitivity," she said, with a tinge of reproach, as she mopped up her eyes with a tissue.

"Not always."

Bonnie Cardoni caught me in the hall on the way to my office.

"You're back on the network," she said. "Sort of."

"What does that mean?"

"I can't get full access."

"To what?" I asked.

"That's the weird part. You're allowed back into the high-level financial reporting, not that you ever went there, according to the logs, but not the detail. Billing, payables, cost-accounting, general ledger, all that stuff is blocked."

"And you can't unblock it."

"Apparently not. So it's either Colin or God."

"No one else?"

"Paresh would have had access, but he wouldn't know how. Though now he's hanging out with God, or whoever Hindus hang out with."

I told her it was no big deal. The last thing I cared about was accounting. Given the funny stuff that went on with corporate finances, originally ascribed to me, it made sense Brice would want to keep me out of those areas. But I couldn't share that with her.

"There's one more thing," she said, before I could move on. She pinched my shirt, gently pulled me into a nearby conference room and shut the door. "You can't get into the employee files either. And you go there a lot."

She conveyed a mix of embarrassment and mild distress. I assured her, again, that this was a minor matter I'd take care of. She seemed nearly relieved, though reluctant to end the conversation, as if another emotion had taken hold.

Alarm.

CHAPTER NINE

The next few weeks were blessedly filled with mountains of work at ExciteAble Technologies. With the help of the increasingly valuable Joey Adams, I ran a continuous series of catch-up meetings with people all over the operation, and where possible, began the process of interrelationship repair. As I moved from meeting to meeting I often encountered Megan Rajput, who never failed to wordlessly flash a big smile.

I was also scheduled to meet with Colin Brice, but for one reason or another, he put the meeting off. It was barely worth noting since he was arguably the busiest person in the company aside from Megan Rajput. But I finally forced the issue by showing up at his office one day when I saw his door was open.

"This still a bad time?" I asked.

He wavered a moment, checking his smartphone, then said to come on in.

"Sorry about this," he said. "I'm just swamped."

"Understandable. There's a lot going on."

"No shit."

We spent some time on basic business, me asking him about his reports and if I could help in any way and getting his overall perspective on company morale and work flow. As always, he had some good insights that I could fold into my schedule. We also booked a regular meeting to help assure we'd stay in steady contact.

Then I asked him about my network access.

"I don't care about the financial details," I said, "and I can understand why that access was blocked, but I do need to get into the employee files. It's part of my job to stay current on changes and add updates of my own. It's been a while and I'm falling behind."

He projected mild surprise, too mild to be credible.

Nevertheless, he said, "Sure, Waters, absolutely. We'll take care of that."

"I appreciate it. Soon, I hope?"

"Absolutely," he said, with more vigor. "You got it."

While not exactly dismissing me, he seemed eager to have me out of his office. So I left, closing the door behind me, at his request.

I settled on what I hoped was a patternless approach to commuting, driving my motorcycle to different train stations, or parking lots close to the office, where I could safely leave it and grab a cab. The sweep for GPS trackers was short and simple on a motorcycle and became part of the routine.

My motel room was occasionally afflicted with noisy overnight neighbors, but thus far, none permanent. I even spent a pleasant evening with the East Indian owners around an outdoor grill where they enjoyed serving me their cultural cuisine and I happily let them do it.

Olivia had gone dark, but that was not unprecedented. I missed her but held to a faith born of experience that a call would come through eventually.

Colin Brice had Bonnie Cardoni rewrite the accounting password every day and log everyone on. They also screwed down malware- and virus-filters and installed card-reader security locks at strategic entrances. It slowed down productivity a little, but no one complained. They also brought in overnight security patrols that watched the parking lot during the late shifts and recorded the license plates of cars in the visitors' section near the front door. New security cameras recorded all comings and goings throughout the operation.

Megan signed off on all of it, without asking me, which I found encouraging.

Eventually, it felt like equilibrium had been restored, if not the former level of collegial flow, but our products were being made with zero defects and orders filled without delay, and the ship seemed to be on an even keel.

I hadn't heard from the killer for a while, so maybe that made me feel okay about going back to Skinny McDowell's for dinner and a few beers. Most of the regulars were there, and to their credit, didn't immediately comment on Paresh and what had been reported in the media, limited as it was.

I got through my cobb salad and doubled-up Scotch before Professor Bowdin, late in his Bourbon budget, ventured a thought on the matter.

"Been having a bit of a time lately, haven't we," he said.

"We have," I said. "Can't talk about it, of course."

"Of course." He took a sip. "I met Rajput."

"Really."

"He spoke at the university. Why would a linguist want to hear a talk by a tech guru, you might ask. No reason. I went out of boredom and curiosity. Though I'm glad I did."

"Smart guy."

"Indeed. It was standing room only. Our students hoping some of his commercial brilliance would sprinkle down on them from the podium."

"And the professors?" I asked.

"Jealousy, and an opportunity to feel morally superior, their favorite sport. Though Rajput never gave them the chance. He spoke of the uplifting power of technology to transform the well-being of all people, even those like him born in grinding poverty in some sweltering village in India. That was true, I hope."

I said it was. His childhood probably worse than he expressed.

Overhearing our conversation, the fire chief asked if the cops were going to catch the bastard. Since I honestly didn't know, I just said they were working on it. Not unfamiliar with the trials of law enforcement, he understood what I meant. A tough case.

From there the conversations returned to the usual ebb and flow of banalities and worthless, though entertaining, observations on sports teams and current events. Like my hours in the gym and congenial meetings at the office, the normalcy of the moment was a salve, a reminder that I could still have an existence outside one of existential terror and unrelenting vigilance.

When I originally left the condo, I set up a post office box to receive my mail. I picked it up every two or three days, retrieving bills and important notices and tossing the rest in the trash.

That day I had a letter with no return address, with a regular canceled stamp. Usually a direct mail come-on, I opened it anyway just to be sure. It read:

"Dear Waters:
    You probably thought you could hide from me, but now you know that just isn't possible. See you around."

He was right, of course. It wasn't possible to be invisible and function as a professional person with manifold duties and responsibilities. The best I could hope for was to make it harder for him, slow him down. And in a perverse way, make things more interesting. More of a challenge. Which might in turn tempt him into taking greater risks, and maybe leaving a footprint of his own.

I brought the letter over to Detective Shapiro. He seemed glad to see me, though all he had to share was an apology.

"I got nothin', Waters," he said, as we sat in the two chairs in front of the desk in his tiny office. "Nothing on the notes, phone traces, the cherry bombs, the GPS tracker, or from the forensics on your condo, car, or storage unit. Our killer is very, very careful."

"Any thoughts on how he got into my hotel room?"

"We have an embarrassed concierge."

"Really."

"According to the key record, she let herself into your room about thirty minutes after you left to go to dinner. We know that's not what actually happened, because at that exact time she was delivering a bouquet of roses and a complimentary bottle of wine to some toff on the concierge level who couldn't get his wallet, checkbooks, and passport out of the safe, and neither could security, meaning the safe guys had to come and several hours later got it open. Said toff, a frequent overcharged customer, was not amused."

"The killer boosted her master key," I said.

"He did. We're not sure when, since she hadn't used it for a few days, not noticing that it wasn't in the usually highly secure, foolproof containment chamber, aka the top drawer of her desk, which was in the hospitality suite on that same level."

"No security cameras in the suite," I said.

"No. It's supposed to be for the exclusive use of the fancy-asses on that floor, but they rarely check."

"Still, it took some ingenuity to know such a thing was possible."

"For a guy who can open the four-digit combination lock on your storage unit, this was child's play."

"But it proved there really was someone other than me who could have done this. Which is why you let me go."

"It is. But don't get too comfortable. You still could have set up the whole thing."

"What about other security cameras around the hotel?"

"They don't have them in the hallways. Only everywhere else—external and food service entrances, porte cochere, lobby, front desk, at the elevator landings, and around the parking lot. And that's just for guests. If you're an employee, you can pretty much assume they watch your every move. Food and liquor storage, service areas, loading docks. I've got copies here, which you're welcome to look at if you have a few spare days. I don't know what you'd be able to see. Just a lot of people coming and going. Our killer would know how to never show his face."

"What about guest IDs? Can you check them out?"

"We did, and they're all legit. Was one of them the killer? No way. He'd never check in under his own name, given all his clever, clever ways. And I mean clever. I don't think I'd be able to pull all this shit off, and I'm, like, a trained professional."

"Focus and preparation," I said. "If I told you to quit your job and spend a year mounting a similar operation, you could do it. What looks random to us is all just careful planning."

Shapiro got up from his chair and went over to a file cabinet. After shuffling through some files, he pulled out an eight-by-ten black-and-white photo. It was a grainy portrait of a scruffy guy with tiny features and half-lidded eyes.

"Twenty-year FBI agent turned mob hit man for another ten. Knew every trick in the book. Never apprehended, unless you count scraping his remains off the sidewalk after the competition emptied a twelve-gauge into his midriff at point blank range."

"So the killer could be professionally trained," I said.

"Can't rule it out. People like to say criminals are stupid. I don't subscribe to that as a generality. The prisons have plenty of people who'd be running corporations if life had taken a few different turns. More often, it's just a lack of knowledge, and admittedly, some trouble with impulse control. The rarest bird of all is a smart, educated, disciplined individual on a mission."

"Like the killer."

"Yeah, that guy."

Olivia finally surfaced soon after that. Her coded text message to my cell phone suggested a meet-up in Manhattan, where business was bringing her for a series of interviews with potential recruits. I said sure and selected a night.

The pattern was to start out at a restaurant a few blocks south of Grand Central, the end of the New Haven Line. I stuffed a few overnight necessities into a backpack and drove the Harley down to West Haven, where I grabbed the train and two hours later was striding through the swirling hordes of commuters and bedazzled tourists, walking my way to an Italian restaurant a half story below the sidewalk, where all street sounds were subdued, and the temperature was slightly too cold in the summer, too hot in the winter, and the food fell short of perfection only by being too plentiful.

Olivia was at our preferred table with a goblet of red wine and wearing a dress that expressed the Platonic ideal of herself. She was in animated conversation with our favorite waiter who looked happy to have someone eager to converse. He seemed glad to see me as well, since we had our own rapport, cultivated over frequent dinners and larger than average tips.

"Would the mister like his usual Scotch on the rocks?" he said.

"The mister would indeed. When you get a chance."

He said the chance was upon us and slipped away.

"Damn, you're handsome," said Olivia.

"You just think that because you haven't seen me for a while. Let me know your thoughts after the night matures."

She sat back in her chair and took a sip of wine.

"The correct response is 'And you're beautiful.'"

"You know you're beautiful. Why bother with all that needless reinforcement?"

"I can never tell if you're a highly refined intellectual or an insensitive thug."

"They aren't the same thing?"

As the drinks were being assembled and delivered, we pulled our chairs closer together so we could better hear each other and more subtly touch. I was surprised to realize how much I needed that touch and found myself indulging in highly risky behaviors like sweeping her hair back off her forehead and picking lint off the silky black dress.

She didn't try to stop me.

"I'm recruiting for a job that could reach into the seven-figure range after options and bonuses," she said. "Interested?"

"Not really. I live in a small place. Not enough room for all that money."

"The funny thing is, I think you'd be a good choice. You'd just have to spiff up the social skills."

"Sorry. That's a deal breaker."

She asked me how it was coming with my murderous stalker, and I told her nowhere, which choked off that line of conversation. I made up for it by telling her how I was integrating back into the company and the challenges that came with that. This talk fell loosely into her area of expertise, leading her to share her own experiences, so it saw us through the rest of dinner.

Over brandy she wrote a number on a napkin.

"Give me a half hour head start," she said. "I need to powder my nose and send off a few e-mails. Not necessarily in that order."

I gave her fifteen minutes, and her nose still looked fine. We took it from there.

———— • ————

WHEN I got back late the next day, Megan Paresh told me Nelson Sarnac had handed her an informal offer to buy our company for three and a half times gross yearly revenue, in a cash deal, with no strings attached. Supposedly.

She tried to look calm about it, but her face was red enough to overwhelm most of the freckles.

"Do you know how much money that is?" she asked.

"My math skills are sketchy, but I think about a hundred and forty million."

"This is what you wanted me to do," she said.

"I did. Now I'm not so sure."

"Jesus Christ."

"Nobody starts out with their best offer," I said. "Certainly not Sarnac. He's low balling."

"Really?"

"He knows something we don't. You could take it and be set for life, but then learn later you left a bundle on the table. How would that make you feel?" I asked.

"Lucky? I don't know. How much do I need? I'm already okay if we just shut the doors tomorrow."

"I have a suggestion."

"I hoped you would."

"Flat-out refuse."

"Easy for you to say."

"You need to buy time to find out what he knows that we don't. Play the emotional card. The company was your late husband's legacy. Can't be bought for any price. Make him think you're irrational. He'll underestimate you. You're so much smarter than he thinks. That's an advantage."

The look on her face was too complicated to interpret. What you'd expect from a woman you'd simultaneously offended and complimented in the same breath.

"Do you really think I'm smarter than people think?"

"Yes," I said, holding her eyes.

"Okay. Good plan."

Chapter Ten

There are fewer lonelier places on earth than a train platform late at night. I'd taken a cab to a station just beyond New Haven, so I could go to the next station and grab my motorcycle. It was a cool night, and I had my hands in the pockets of my sport coat and my mind entangled in all the intricate machinations of my job, compromised love life, and unidentified tormentor.

So I could be excused for not noticing that a large man in an exercise outfit, including a hooded sweatshirt, had also come on the platform. I only realized he was there when he grabbed me by the hair and pulled back my head, then stuck a hard fist into my right kidney.

The pain was so abrupt and profound that it stopped my breath. I went down on my knees, and likely yelled something, or maybe just squawked a little. The next blow was delivered to my right ear, which completely disrupted my cognitive functions, though with much less pain than you'd expect. Even then, I chalked it up to shock, and set myself to the task of getting back on my feet and turning around to face my attacker.

He let me do it, which I took as overconfidence, along with a desire for the semblance of a fair fight, which he'd already negated with the sucker punches. Whatever the reason, I got to move back a few steps and fix my addled eyesight on his looming shape.

The next swing of his fist was committed, but slow. I ducked down and turned a little, absorbing the blow on my upper back. This put me close in to his body, where I really wanted to be. I pushed off the balls of my feet and managed to wrap my arms around his lower torso. I picked him up and used my weight to slam him to the ground.

That worked well enough, though my face hit first, and I could feel the heat of a bad bruise, at the very least, rising on my cheekbone.

He was a big man, with plenty of abdominal muscle, and I had no finesse as a fist fighter, but I knew how to wrestle—an ability successful wrestlers secretly believed conveyed magical advantages in a brawl. That belief was about to be tested.

I had a simple strategy, keep him in a bear hug and squeeze like hell. He continued to hit me on the back and shoulders, but the angle was bad for an effective punch. I took a few deep breaths and drove myself to increase the pressure. He tried to grab my head, but it was too buried in his chest for him to get a solid grip, so he started to punch it instead. But again, the angle of attack was in my favor, and I have a very hard head.

My reasons for all the hours in the gym building muscle had nothing to do with being strong, but now I was glad for that side benefit, because I discovered reserves I never knew I had. All it took was a full breath of air, followed by a tightening of the vice. After a few minutes of this, his strength began to falter, and while he offered no plea for mercy, or even the chance to negotiate, we both knew instinctively that a deepening embrace would likely snap his spine.

I kept squeezing, charged by the primal instinct to kill or be killed.

He stopped clawing at my head, or landing feeble punches, and started to gasp. I realized that my shoulder, pressed into his diaphragm, was exacting the greater toll, essentially choking off his breath. So I twisted around and applied even greater pressure to that part of his body, until even the rasping, labored breaths faded away.

I let go and stood up, dizzy from the exertion and punch to the head. After I gained my balance I knelt down to see if he was dead, or just out cold, an important distinction. I felt around his neck for a pulse and found one. And he was breathing again—shallow, grunting breaths.

I dug out my phone and called Detective Shapiro.

———— • ————

THE ER doc said I'd probably be pissing blood for a while, but the kidney would recover. As would my brain from what might be a mild concussion. He offered me prescription painkillers, but I demurred.

I took a cab to the train station where I'd left my Harley, which I rode back to the motel. I checked the in-room safe to be sure the little automatic was still there, as I did whenever I came home, offering the universe gratitude that I hadn't been carrying that night, which would have provided my opponent quick and easy salvation.

By now it was well after midnight, and all it took was a single beer and some Advil to knock me out until the next morning.

A call from Detective Shapiro woke me up.

"Know a guy named Mike Wojcik?"

"I don't think so."

"He's currently a guest of ours here at New Haven lockup. He's insisting you called him some dirty names and pushed him, forcing him to defend himself."

"That's curious, since my recollection is he attacked me from behind without provocation."

"That's our contention as well, based on clear evidence from the security cams on the train platform. Send a nice thank you note to Big Brother. We're about to give Wojcik an interview. He hasn't lawyered up yet, thank God. Thought you might want to watch in the observation room. And call in sick. Or better yet, I'll have one of our people here call your boss pretending they're from some hospital. We'll say you've been injured and can't come to work. They'll want more information, we'll deflect."

"You're a mensch, Shapiro."

"That's what I keep telling my wife."

———— • ————

ANDY PETTIGREW joined me in the observation room, which had a monitor fed by cameras in a room where they interviewed suspects. We were joined by Shapiro's lieutenant and another detective I'd met before but didn't know very well. They were both cordial enough, in a stiff, professional way. The detective was young, and likely new to the job. Deferential to Pettigrew, which I took as a positive sign.

We watched as Wojcik was brought in. He showed little affect, either in his movements, which were slow and deliberate, or his expression. After sitting down, he stared straight ahead.

Shapiro came in ten minutes later.

"Hey, do you want anything, coffee, water, anything like that?" Shapiro asked.

"A beer would be good."

"A definite possibility, though I'm going to want one, too, and I have to concentrate. We used to hand out cigarettes, but the freaking city banned all that."

"I don't smoke."

"Wise choice. Me neither. My old man used to smoke like a chimney. The stink in the house cured me forever." Wojcik didn't react to that. "So, I see you live in New Britain. And grew up there. Good town."

"Good enough. Changed a lot. Full of Puerto Ricans now. Okay people, just not my type."

"Yeah? What type of people do you like?"

"I don't know. White people. When do I get out of here?"

"Soon. I just want to make sure you get a chance to tell your side of the story. That's all."

"I already told it to them other cops."

"I know. But I'm, like, the boss cop, and I need to make sure they got it right. You sure you don't want anything to drink?"

Wojcik ordered up a cup of black coffee, which Shapiro left the room to get, conveying the fiction that the two of them were the only people involved in the conversation. He came back with a cup for Wojcik and one for himself.

"So," Shapiro said, "this guy was acting like a jerk." Wojcik perked up and leaned forward, as if eager to tell the tale.

"Yeah, exactly. I'm just walkin' along looking at my phone and I sort of brush by him a little bit there on the platform. I say, 'Sorry man,' and he says, like under his breath, 'Douche bag.' I'm thinkin', really, I just hardly touch you and you call me a douche bag? But I let it go, because it's not worth it, you know? I got better things to do than jostle with some dick in fancy clothes at a fucking train station."

"He was wearing fancy clothes?"

"You know, dressy clothes. Some office shit."

"I get it. Then what happened?"

"I tell him something like, 'You oughta be more polite when somebody apologizes.' This seems to piss the guy off, for some reason, and he comes over to me and says something like, 'You oughta watch where you're walking.' I mean, what the fuck? So I get a little close to him, so he knows I'm serious, and say, 'Back off, dick head.' This is when he gives me a little shove." He sat back in his chair, looking self-righteous. "I'm sorry, if you make physical contact, you've just crossed a line. Where I come from, a little shove is notice that something bigger is on its way. So I get preemptive and sock him in the head. You'd do the same thing," he added.

"I probably would. Did he sock you back?"

"Yeah, he did. Then got me into this Kung-Fu hold that oughta be illegal, cause it makes you go blank. I should sue the bastard. Maybe I will."

Shapiro let a little silence build in the room, then said, "I know everything you just told me is a lie. So I don't want to waste any more time talking about what happened. I just want to know why you did it."

Wojcik looked thrown by that.

"You're believing him? That fuck?"

"Security cameras recorded the entire encounter. If you're going to make a living carrying out assaults, you might want to get better at it."

Wojcik kept his peace for a moment, then said, "You're lying."

"I can show you the tapes. It won't change anything. More important is why *you're* lying. I think somebody put you up to it. Put you in a bad spot. I'm thinking your financial situation isn't too great these days. You owe some money?"

Wojcik didn't exactly deflate, but his shoulders fell a little.

"Everybody's got bills," he said.

"Yeah, but not like yours. Bastards really got the squeeze on you, right? And here's an opportunity to get 'em off your back. Look, I know. Cops don't make shit. Try explaining to my wife that I can't just order up a raise. You know the situation, right?"

Wojcik put two balled fists on the table.

"I take care of my own," he said.

"Of course, you do. Any real man would. So, who's putting on the pressure? I hear a lot about these types of guys who sucker you in with a loan, or something else, and then act like they own you. Real sons of bitches."

Wojcik shook his head.

"Nothing like that. I don't even know what you're talking about."

Shapiro leaned across the table.

"Yes, you do," he said. "You're looking at a very serious ticket to shit town for assault and battery. The worst kind. You think you got bills now? Wait till a bunch of years go by cooling your ass in prison. It doesn't have to be that way. Tell me who paid you to do it and the DA can turn that ugly possibility into a slap on the wrist. Otherwise, I walk out of here and you're floating down the proverbial creek without a paddle. Do you understand me?"

Wojcik didn't say anything, but it appeared to me he understood. He was just trying to measure up the pluses and minuses.

"I got a call," he said.

Shapiro gently moved himself into a more comfortable position.

"What kind of call?"

"The kind where a guy says another guy shorted him on a big deal and needed convincing it was time to make it right."

"You knew the caller?"

Wojcik shook his head.

"No. He just told me he knew I occasionally handled this sort of thing. Don't know where he got that. I'm just a guy. Honestly, you can check. The worst thing on my record is a DUI, and that was five years ago."

I looked over at the lieutenant in the room with me, and he nodded.

"What did he offer you?" Shapiro asked.

"Five big ones right away, another five after it was done. Just a little roughing up. Enough to get the guy's attention, but no permanent damage. How was I to know the fucker was some kind of weird martial arts dude? I think he broke one of my ribs."

"You did worse than that to him. He might've taken you down, but right now they got tubes and wires stuck in him so they can pluck out his kidney. Meanwhile, you're walking around all hale and hearty."

Wojcik couldn't hide that this was a satisfying bit of news.

"Okay, so much for nothing permanent," he said.

"I guess he'll let you keep the first five hundred. You did get it, right?"

"Showed up in my mailbox. Cash. A good faith gesture you don't see much these days. Not that I ever done anything like this before," he quickly added.

The lieutenant looked unconvinced.

"So you never saw him, or got his name?" Shapiro asked.

"Hell, no. That's all there is. There ain't nothin' else. Am I going down for this? If that's the case, I need a lawyer."

"Are you asking for a lawyer?"

"I'm asking if I'm going down for this."

"I don't know. I have to ask my boss."

"Okay. Go ask."

Shapiro came into the observation room to ask what we thought. Pettigrew said he bought the guy's story, mostly. It was obvious to all of us he had a little career going in the personal persuasion business, but seriously low rent. Enough to catch the notice of the killer, but nothing beyond that.

The lieutenant wanted to book him and take him off the streets. Turn an easy collar into a solid conviction. Check the success box. That killed the mood since he was the senior guy in the room.

"I respectfully disagree," I said. "I'd kick him. Make him look like a hero, then keep an eye on him, tap his phone, drive by his house. He's the only human we know who's had contact with the killer, besides me. That's big. The killer's smart and skillful, but his choice of Wojcik was amateurish, which means he's not connected with a larger criminal enterprise. Otherwise, I'd be on life support at Yale-New Haven. Or dead. It's the first point of vulnerability that we've seen."

To the lieutenant's credit, he listened. Then he put it to Pettigrew, who agreed with me.

"I think he's worth more to us on the street. If Waters is cool with that, why not?" he said.

Shapiro chimed in.

"I made him think Waters was badly injured. This gives Wojcik some credibility with the killer. Which, with any luck, will keep the connection intact. Something we might be able to exploit. It's a long shot, but it's all we got."

The lieutenant nodded.

"Okay. Kick him. But we don't have the resources to stay on him 24/7." He looked over at Shapiro. "Try to get some cooperation."

"Roger that, chief."

We watched Shapiro go back into the interview room, where he spun his chair around and sat backward, cowboy style. Wojcik stayed rigid in his own chair, his face alert and wary.

"I got a deal for you," said Shapiro. "A one-time only, literally get-out-of-jail-free card. A press release is going out tomorrow. It'll say the guy you jumped was badly beaten on a train platform. That should give what you need to collect the next five hundred. You know where I'm going with this. When your client contacts you again, let us know about it. We might know anyway, since we'll be monitoring your every move, phone call, e-mail, letter, yodel in the valley. Like Santa Claus, we'll know if you've been sleeping, we'll know if you're taking a shit. So for goodness sake, don't fuck with us."

"I can do that. I don't care about this motherfucker."

"I'm glad to hear that, because honestly, we care deeply about you."

"Sure. Go fuck yourself."

"Roger that."

CHAPTER ELEVEN

My request for some time off was an easy sell since Detective Shapiro did a convincing job of describing my battered condition. Too convincing, since I got a somewhat panicked call from Megan Paresh and had to assure her that in a few days I'd be fit as a fiddle and ready to assume my full responsibilities.

Despite the swollen ear, sore kidney, and giant scrape on my face, I was already fit enough, but I had plans for the free time.

New Britain, Connecticut, was about an hour north of my motel. An old mill town, with a big Polish population that once kept the hardware and fabrication factories churning, the place still had a sturdy middle-class feel to it, even as poorer Latinos flowed into town and mingled with the Poles.

Mike Wojcik owned a house near Broad Street, in a neighborhood within walking distance of the Polish retail district. The real estate was modest, but well-kept. Mostly single-story homes, with economy imports and trucks in the driveways and parked along the street. I risked a single pass on the motorcycle to get my bearings. A pickup was in the driveway, which didn't mean anyone was home. I knew Wojcik had a wife and some kids, not sure how many or how old. I took in what I could as I rolled past, and rode to the edge of downtown, at the first cluster of storefronts, bars, and coffee shops.

I sat at the counter of a claustrophobic diner that was likely remodeled sometime in the Eisenhower era. The newest thing in the place was a white board with specials of the day written in erasable marker. I ordered off the food-stained menu from a wiry woman in her late fifties. Her hands were crooked and her hair closely resembled No. 2 steel wool. She called me hon, which I took as an invitation to have a friendly tête-à-tête.

"A number three, please," I said.

"Excellent choice."

"Can you throw some cheese in the scrambled eggs?" I asked.

"Excellent choice."

"Butter on the wheat toast? And add some fried ham?"

"Another excellent choice."

She wrote down the order, then asked me what the other guy looked like, pointing at the contusion on my cheek.

"Better than me, but I won the fight."

"That doesn't surprise me, lookin' at the size of you."

"Size isn't everything. You also need technique."

She liked that very much.

"My husband used to have both, but the arthritis got to him. On disability, like all his friends from the plant."

I threw out the name of one of the bigger factories in town, still running, though at less than a quarter of prior strength.

"Yeah, you work there?" she asked.

I shook my head.

"Just when I was a kid," I said, which was true. "Now I'm pulling wire for the electrical company. I like your place. Seen it all my life, never came in."

She looked around the counter to make sure other customers weren't trying to flag her down. Then she leaned into me and said, "It's a piece of shit, but at least it's my piece of shit. You want coffee?"

After I got through the meal, she stopped by again to clear the counter and give me the check.

"My back porch is falling in and I'm looking for some help to put it back in shape," I said.

Shapiro had given me Wojcik's card. I slid it across the counter. "Do you know this guy?"

She studied it.

"There're lots of Wojciks around here, but I don't know this one. My cousin's a carpenter. I can put you in touch."

She came back with my change and her cousin's phone number written on an unused check. I thanked her.

"He works slow, but he's honest and does a decent job. And could really use the work," she said. "If you want to talk to him face-to-face, he's over at the library putting in a new front door."

I thanked her again and went outside to look up the New Britain Public Library on my smartphone. It only took a few minutes to get there, despite the tangle of one-way streets and construction, obstacles made less so on a motorcycle that could cut through parking lots and slip down narrow walkways.

I parked the bike and walked around until I saw a crew at the front entrance of the original building, an elegant neoclassic so massive and stolid I wondered if there was any room left for books.

The entrance was cut off by yellow safety tape and a little work site was down on the lawn. I walked over there. I asked the first guy I came to if the boss was nearby. He pointed to the top of the stairs where a tradesman in a tan jumpsuit with long, grey hair pulled back in a headband, was working a cutoff saw. I approached cautiously, to avoid startling him.

When he spotted me, he pulled back from the saw with a freshly cut piece of mahogany in his hand. I said his cousin from the diner had given me his name. He brightened up.

"What did you eat?" he asked.

"A number three."

"Excellent choice."

I told him about my back porch and that I was getting bids on the repair. I already had one from a guy named Mike Wojcik and wondered if he knew his work. I handed him Wojcik's card. He looked at it and handed it back.

"I can't beat him on price," he said. "I do actual carpentry."

"What does he do?"

"Butchery. He could do the demolition. Good with a chain saw and sledgehammer. But I wouldn't want him putting on a new porch. Don't tell him I said that."

"Why's that?" I asked him.

"I don't need to make enemies. Especially not a hothead like Wojcik."

"Tough guy, huh?"

"Likes to think so," he said. "You look like you went a few rounds yourself, if you don't mind me saying so."

"I don't mind. I started to tear down that porch myself and whacked my own face with a two-by-four. Decided then and there to get some help."

We talked a bit more about the hazards of deconstruction, and I asked him to describe the difference between real tradesmen and a handyman like Wojcik.

"I'm not talking against anybody," he said, "you just need to know what you're getting into." He flipped the piece of mahogany up in the air and caught it again. "And if I was you, I'd drop it."

"Drop what?"

"Gettin' your ass kicked is nothing to be embarrassed about. Especially when it's kicked by a big son of a bitch like Wojcik. If you're looking for revenge, he's the wrong dude to go after."

"How so?"

"He's got friends in bad places. If you start sniffin' around here he'll know about it, and next time it really will be a two-by-four, and you'll never see it coming."

In my team-building training classes, I'd describe a situation like this as a strategic crossroads. A euphemism meant to preserve my trainees' self-esteem, more universally known as a fuckup. Though at least I was learning something, however clumsy the approach.

"Won't know it from you, though, is my guess," I told him.

He gave a faint shake of the head.

"Guy's a meatball. No respect from me. Same with his friends. Punks. Don't mean I go looking for trouble. I'd advise you do the same."

I stuck out my hand, and he took it.

"Thank you. Good advice."

He kept shaking and applying steady pressure. I'd known other carpenters, and they all had forearms like Popeye and strength to match. So for the second time in as many days, I was in a squeezing contest. I countered until I saw him flinch and felt him give up.

"Though if I was looking for trouble," I said, as I let go, "who's the next level up from Wojcik in the food chain?"

He shook out his hand in the air.

"That's quite a grip you got on you," he said. "Must've been a hell of a fight. The guy you're probably talking about is Eddie Kozlowski. Has a plumbing business, but doesn't seem to do a lot of plumbing. Still gets to drive an Escalade. I'm not sure I should be telling you this."

He looked around the jobsite to make sure no one was in earshot.

"No worries from me," I said. "You're a good man. I apologize for approaching you under false pretenses. It's much more embarrassing than getting your face slammed into the pavement. But you gave me a valuable lesson, which I'll never forget."

"Okay," he said, "that's cool. If there really is a porch, I can give you an estimate."

I took a piece of scrap paper out of my pocket and wrote down an e-mail address, which I handed to him.

"No porch. But if you ever get in a jam, write me. I'll help if I can."

He read the address as if it held secret powers. I gave a little wave and started to walk away.

"You a cop?" he called after me.

I turned around and walked backward.

"Psychologist. No better or worse."

I went to a coffee shop where I could use my laptop to get on the Internet. I invested some money in background check websites, most of which were worthless con jobs, but I finally hit one that served up a decent amount of infor-mation on Edward (Koz) Kozlowski: age, address, phone number, names of immediate family, liens, criminal record (assault arrests, no convictions), lawsuits, and published arti-cles (none).

It also gave the address of his plumbing operation, listed as his employer. I went into the bathroom and pulled a wad of bills out of my wallet. Then I rode over there. The busi-ness was in an old manufacturing plant converted into a multiuse industrial park. It took me a while to find the sign, which was barely large enough to read, stuck on the brick wall between a door and a single garage bay.

I tried the door, which was locked. So I rang the bell. The door opened a crack, held by a chain. An eye peered out halfway to the floor. I thought it was a kid at first, before I saw the beard.

"What do you want?" he said, not in a hostile way. As if I might actually want something.

"Information," I said, holding up a hundred-dollar bill.

He took it through the narrow opening and shut the door. For a moment, I thought I was about to learn another object lesson, but the door opened again, still restrained by the chain.

"You a cop?"

"No."

"Press?"

"No. Private citizen. I was told nobody knows what goes on around here better than you."

The door closed again so he could unhook the chain, then opened the rest of the way into a room crammed with metal furniture, though reasonably clean and orderly. Koz moved quickly to a desk chair, which he spun around and stuck in a corner, then used a big, silvery automatic to point at a padded stool on the other side of the room.

My first thought was one of Snow White's elves. Short, round, with a grey beard and bulbous cheeks and nose. The big gun was the only thing that undermined the comparison.

"Take a load off," he said, as he stuffed the hundred in his shirt pocket. "No guarantees I can tell you what you want to know. Who gave you the shiner?" he asked, pointing at my face.

"One of your boys. It's why I'm here."

He got a better grip on the automatic and rested it in his lap.

"I don't have any boys. Just one girl, and she's a college kid who hates me. Blames me for her genes, like I could do anything about that."

"Mike Wojcik jumped me the other night. Somebody paid him to do it. I won the fight, by the way. Just so you know," I added.

"What do I care about Mike Wojcik? Nothing to do with me."

"How much did he pay you?" I asked.

"Who the hell are you talking about?"

"The guy who was looking for muscle. You gave him Wojcik's name. What did the guy pay you?" I took another hundred-dollar bill out of my wallet and tossed it on the floor between us. "I'd hand it to you, but I'm afraid to get too close. You might stick a hole in me with that cannon of yours."

He looked down at the money with an appraising eye.

"He gave me a grand," said Koz, smirking. "Easiest payday of my life."

I rolled the stool back against the wall to rest my back and sore kidney. When I got comfortable, I smiled and shook my head.

"Koz, you're missing an important component here."

He didn't take that well.

"I hate shit like that. People suggesting to me that I'm stupid. I've been dealing with that shit my whole life"— he picked up the gun and pointed it at the middle of my chest—"and at this stage, I don't feel the need to deal with it anymore."

He stared at me and I tried not to look at the spittle that had formed on his lips, a caricature of a rabid dog.

"You're not stupid," I said. "In fact, you're probably smarter than 90 percent of the people you deal with every day. Given your height and unimposing appearance, it's a real accomplishment to have ascended to such a high level within a serious criminal network. I admire you quite a bit."

He relaxed a little, even lowering the gun back to his lap, where he caressed it like it was a purring kitten.

I said, "I'm sorry if I gave offense. What I meant to say is there's a piece of information you're unaware of, through no fault of your own, that you might need to know."

He rocked his head back and forth, and said, "Okay, so what do I need to know so bad that I'm sitting here wasting my time with you?"

I balled my fists and tapped them on my knees, a signal that he should listen to what I had to say.

"The guy's going to kill you."

Koz's face looked confused, with just a touch of alarm.

"What are you talking about?"

"I told you," I said, "I won the fight. Your designated thug blew it. That means you're a dead man."

Koz rearranged himself in his chair, trying to get more comfortable. Throughout, the gun stayed trained on my upper body.

"That ain't my fault," he said, with little contrition. "I just passed along a name. No guarantees."

"The guy you talked to isn't an ordinary guy. He doesn't know the rules, and even if he did, he wouldn't play by them."

I told him how the New Haven cops had decided to spring Wojcik and maintain a fiction that I'd been badly injured and the perpetrator was still on the loose. The hope being the bad guy would reengage with Wojcik and thus expose himself. Unlike my approach with the carpenter, I stuck to the facts, just not all of them.

"As soon as the guy learns the truth about Wojcik's fuckup, you'll lose his trust, and become risk factors. Which means, you and Wojcik are both dead men."

Kozlowski might have been smarter than most, but I wouldn't have placed him anywhere near the genius category. It took him a while to adjust to a new reality.

"If what you're saying is true, how's the guy gonna find out?" he asked.

"As soon as the cops decide Wojcik is a dead end, they charge him, and I testify and that's that."

He got the implication.

"I can't tell you anything. I never seen the guy. He just called me."

"And you just handed over a valuable piece of information with no assurances from him?"

"He used the same assurances you did. Hundred-dollar bills. Ten of them, delivered here by US mail."

"Do you still have the envelope?"

"Shit no," he said, then thought about it. "Yeah, I might, in the dumpster behind the shop. You're welcome to take a look."

"And the phone number he called from."

Koz took out his smartphone and used his thumb to swipe through recent calls. "Here it is," he said. "The number is 'blocked call.'"

"No other contact points?" I asked.

He said no. I asked him a few more questions, but that was all he had. I saw no reason for him to hold out, so I got up to leave.

"If you hear from this guy again—phone, text, e-mail, whatever—call me," I said. "And Wojcik doesn't have to know we had this conversation. In fact, the less you see of him the better."

"Mike Wojcik? Never heard of him."

Before I left, he asked me who this guy was, what he was all about.

"A person with antisocial disorder, coupled with extreme paranoia and all-consuming revenge fantasies."

"Okay," he said. "Whatever the fuck."

Chapter Twelve

I stopped by the motel room for a shower, a necessity after spending a half hour wading through Kozlowski's dumpster, used primarily, it seemed, for disposing of leftover lunch food.

Kozlowski had acted offended by the stink when I brought him the envelope to identify, though his pleasure in my condition was obvious. He was confident I'd found the right one, noting the lack of a return address. And the regular stamps, canceled in Old Saybrook, CT. While the faintest of clues, it was strangely compelling for me to see a tangible bit of evidence. He gave me a larger envelope for transport and told me to get the hell out of there before he had to call the fumigators.

After drying off, I called Shapiro and he was able to meet me at a greasy spoon close to my motel. He looked a little unhappy when he arrived.

"Better if you call me when you get another brainstorm," he said, as he sat at the table. "I'm not big on junior detective work."

It was a close read, but I didn't think he was that concerned, especially since he'd given me Wojcik's contact info, with an implicit permission to take some initiative. I decided the warning was more to establish precedent he could later hide behind.

I handed him the envelope and gave a detailed rundown on the day's activities. I tried to be as accurate and thorough as possible, including both missteps and what I considered effective tactics. Shapiro, offering neither criticism nor praise, simply jotted down notes in a little notebook.

He put on a pair of surgical gloves and slid the envelope out from its protective cover.

"We'll check for prints and DNA, of course, but I wouldn't be hopeful," he said.

"Me neither. But at least we know he mailed it from Old Saybrook. About an hour east of New Haven."

Shapiro took out his cell phone and tapped it for a few moments.

"Tell me that's not nothing," I said.

"It's not nothing, it's just not much. We assume our boy is pretty local. Too much busy work in the area. At least he's not working out of Wisconsin or something. Be tough on our travel budget."

"Do you think he'll connect again with Wojcik or Kozlowski?" I asked.

He shrugged.

"Maybe, but I doubt it. Not enough benefit to justify the risk."

"Can you bug their phones?"

He looked at me with the indulgence one reserves for six-year-olds and golden retrievers.

"Number one, we don't have the resources—time or money—to justify the effort. Warrants, technology, staff utilization, department priorities, etc., etc. Number two, we don't have the time or money."

"So if he does, we have to hope the New Britain dopes will call it in," I said.

"That is the low-cost, confidential informant approach. If that happens, we'll have something to work with. Maybe."

He called over a waitress and ordered breakfast. I joined him, asking for eggs and ham, wheat bread with two tabs of butter. I told her to just pile it on one plate.

"More efficient," I told Shapiro.

"My wife would never let me do that."

"More the reason to stay single."

Some time passed while he absorbed that, then changing the subject, asked, "So explain something to me. We both know that establishing a connection with the killer is the only way we're going to draw him in, yet you seem to be working mighty hard to avoid connecting."

"You've obviously never been a teenage girl playing hard to get. The more she acts disinterested, the more he tries to get her attention. It forces him to be more creative, since he still hopes she'll eventually find him appealing. In this case, maintaining just enough distance, and just enough control over what's possible, reduces the amount of satisfaction he can derive from provoking and harassing me, which is the point of the game. The hope is that this will force the killer into taking greater risks as he tries to gain more control, and thus greater satisfaction."

"So you went back to work, which creates greater exposure, but you're hiding the rest of the time."

"Hiding is an okay word, though I think of it as a strategic denial of access. Balanced by turning my smartphone back on and exposing myself on the job, an important choice, since I don't know if the killer is involved with the company. For all I know, I say hello to him every day."

Shapiro said he understood and accepted the logic and thanked me for the insight.

"I can see why Pettigrew likes you," he said.

"Oh?"

"You're a good man to have in the room."

My smartphone chirped at me as we sat at the table, signaling that a voice message was waiting. I left Shapiro to his meal and when I was back in the parking lot I listened to the message while sitting on the Harley.

"I hope your recovery is going slowly," said the mechanical voice. "It means you'll have time to have a little talk."

A new text had also come in. It was from Unknown Number and contained only the URL of a chat room website. I was tempted to forward it to Detective Shapiro, but decided that was premature. I needed time to calculate the proper course of action. Whether to withhold or disclose, a decision I never took lightly.

The site was called Chatjazz, and it was free and accessible from anywhere in the world. There was no registration, nor request for identification. You just chose a user name, and provided gender, age, city, and country. All on the honor system, and thus entirely anonymous to other users, though not entirely to the site, depending on how good you were at disguising your IP address.

I logged on as ExciteAble Boy, with my correct age and city, making it as easy as possible for him to find me through the search function. My first post was, "Recovery better than expected. Ready to talk."

Since there were no alerts, I checked the site every few hours for the next week, until I finally got an answer. By then, I was back at ExciteAble, and distracted by the mountain of work I was still digging through, so I got a small jolt when I read the words, "Last time I send a Polack to do a man's work."

It was posted by "Plato."

I waited another week to respond: "Cowards of all ethnicities are not men."

"Sc**w you," he wrote back immediately, written to avoid violating the site's anti-obscenity provision. Rather than answering, I called Detective Shapiro and told him about my new friend on Chatjazz.

"You were supposed to tell me about any material event in this case," he said.

"It wasn't material until the connection was clear and certain. Can we trace it?"

"We can't, but maybe the FBI can. I'll take a walk over there soon as I finish my lunch. Corn beef and rye, with just a little bit of mustard."

"Bon appétit."

———— • ————

COLIN BRICE sent me an e-mail, with an apology for taking so long to restore my network access to the employee files. He said to just go ahead and log on as I usually did, and to let him know if there were any problems.

All seemed in order. I spent a few hours cross-checking my recent projects with employee participants, bringing their files up to date where necessary. I dropped a commendation letter in Joey Adams's file, and planned to do the same for Colin Brice, but then had my first surprise.

His file wasn't there. Not blocked, just not there. I searched for those of other senior managers and counted all present. Then, on a hunch, I went to the archives that held past employees, and found another conspicuous absence.

Yolanda Alexander. Our former failed CFO. Colin Brice's predecessor.

Later that afternoon I got a text from Olivia Lefèvre. It had been a long drought, long enough that I was beginning to think she was bowing out of the relationship. That brought on sad thoughts, which I nearly managed to repress, so when the text came, I was unusually lifted at the sight of Sinclair Importing on the little screen.

"Been in Paris for a few weeks. Didn't trust security of communications. Sorry."

"Welcome back," I wrote.

"Taking train into the city on Wednesday. Can you join me?"

"Delighted. Name the time and save me a seat."

"Returning Thursday?" she wrote.

"I would hope so."

I remember my brother, reuniting with his girlfriend after a similarly long hiatus, coming into my room and saying, in a thick Irish brogue, "Laddy, me heart is soarin' like a hawk." For the first time, I really understood what he meant.

It was a simple plan. She got on the 7:20 A.M. out of Union Station in New Haven, which was nearly empty, so she had her choice of seats. I got on in West Haven, ten minutes down the track, and walked through the cars until I found her, dressed like a banker, with her blonde hair pulled back so tightly it looked painted on. I sat down.

"Bonjour, Mademoiselle."

"Monsieur. You've lost weight."

"You've become even more beautiful. Though it might be the makeup."

"Good call. They got some crazy good makeup wizards over there in France."

"That sounds like an excellent marketing strategy for a line of cosmetics: 'Crazy Good French Wizards For Your Face.'"

"How'd you get the bruise under your eye? You could use those wizards."

"My face was shoved into the ground by a big guy in a sweat suit."

"Did you shove back?"

"No. But I did squeeze him until his eyes nearly popped out of his head."

"Tell me the rest of the story. We're stuck with each other for at least the next two hours."

So I did, as thoroughly as memory would allow. And since I had an excellent memory, it took nearly the whole two hours to exhaust the story. She listened attentively, and only interrupted by touching my face and a spot within the vicinity of my right kidney, then drifting from there.

"How is it working?" she asked.

"All systems go. Pissing like a racehorse."

"I hope you're being careful. I'd really rather not lose you."

"I'd rather not lose me either, but being too careful will just prolong the situation, ruin what joy I have in life, and undermine our ability to catch this son of a bitch."

As always, the train filled rapidly as we stopped at stations toward the end of the line. With so many ears in direct proximity, we switched the conversion to her time in Paris. My experience with the city amounted to a three-day visit during a post-college swing through Europe, so she did most of the talking.

"You need to go again," she said. "See what's changed and what hasn't. Next time I'll take you with me."

"I'll just need a passport."

"Let's eat French tonight. It'll be a good warmup."

After booking separate rooms at the hotel, we had a few hours before Olivia was to interview a promising candidate. We spent the time walking around the immediate neighborhood at a somewhat quicker pace than we wanted, hoping to avoid being mowed down by resolute, fast-walking New Yorkers. I asked her why she was looking at my feet.

"You don't step on the cracks in the sidewalk," she said. "I've never noticed that before. Are you afraid of breaking your mother's back?"

"No. If you step on a crack, bears emerge from the manhole covers and eat you. I discovered this in childhood reading A. A. Milne. Never actually happened, but I see no reason to abandon the practice."

"You're an interesting man, Waters."

" 'Interesting' is the word most frequently used to damn with faint praise."

"Is that true, or are you making it up?"

"Simple observation," I said. "I don't need a scientific study to confirm what my experience shows to be demonstrably true. For example, I've never once observed you express a falsehood to me, or even allow a misapprehension to stand uncorrected. You obviously know how to lie, otherwise we wouldn't be here together. But I've never known you to lie to me. I find great comfort in that."

"Because you value trust?"

"Because perceiving lies can be exhausting."

"You perceive that many?"

"All day long."

As planned, we found a French restaurant that specialized in the type of Parisian cuisine Olivia had become accustomed to. It was lit in a way that improved the look of the customers' complexions, though made reading the menu nearly impossible. The place was so small it could barely seat two dozen people, though the price per meal probably made the economics still work out in their favor.

"Bring us whatever you think is good," Olivia told the waiter, an approach that rendered the menu irrelevant, thus keeping cost out of consideration until the bill came.

I asked her if that was what she always did.

"In Paris, yes. Food to the French is art. If you want a painter to do his best work, you don't direct his brushstrokes."

"It must result in some surprising meals."

"You bet. There's no part of any living thing that the French don't find inviting."

As a child, I once survived for an entire year on nothing but burger meat and baked beans. I don't know what effect this had on my development, though the damage apparently wasn't long-lasting. Learning to eat food that disgusted me, which was everything but burger and beans, was one of my first self-improvement projects. Since nothing tasted good, and had to be forced down, all things organic were on the menu, just like in France. Consequently, when my palate was finally beaten into submission, there was nothing I couldn't eat. Though I did take a long break from burger and beans.

I shared all this with Olivia, and seeing the merriment the story was producing, I milked it through all three courses. Thus we were in the process of choosing between the lavender sorbet and the papaw and passion fruit panna cotta when Erik with a K pulled up a chair.

"Hi, Olivia."

She jumped an inch and put her hand to her throat.

"Erik. You startled me."

His smile was all mouth and no eyes, which were a shade of pale blue I'd only seen in Alaskan dogs. The effect was exaggerated by his black hair, too black to be entirely natural, and slicked back with something that added a glossy sheen. None of these features matched my mind's eye image of him, completely contrived, since I'd never seen his photo, and Olivia had never described him to me.

She told me he was her husband, and introduced me, without hesitation, by my real name. Though there was the barest tremor in her voice. His handshake was dry, and neutral, neither fish-like nor competitive.

"Olivia has been good enough to consider me for a new opportunity," I said. "She thought picking up the tab at a fancy French restaurant was a fair exchange."

"Erik, what the hell are you doing here, and how did you find me?"

"I'm a certified private investigator," he said, looking at me. "Piece of cake. And you're not the only one who gets to go to New York City," he added, looking back at her with a widening smile.

He asked me what I did for a living, and I told him management consulting. The open position was VP of operations, though I needed to honor the arrangement with Olivia's employer not to reveal the company's name.

"I can understand that," he said. "Smart VPs need to know how to keep their mouths shut."

Olivia said we were about to order dessert and asked if he wanted anything to eat, or drink, signaling to our waiter, who was gracious when we passed on dessert after all and asked for coffee instead. Olivia asked if they had light cream and Splenda, saying coffee was unbearable without it.

Erik ordered a gin and tonic with two shots of gin, no lime.

"I like what you did with your hair," he said to Olivia. "Explains why you took so long in the bathroom this morning."

"I hope I didn't wake you. I tried to be quiet as a mouse."

"You were. I'm just a light sleeper. Comes with the cop brain."

Olivia explained that he'd spent twenty years with the NYPD before going private, ten of those years split between undercover and homicide. Erik told her not to forget being loaned out to the FBI in a political corruption case in Connecticut, which introduced him to our state. A big case everyone thought they knew about. He said to picture bags of money being stuffed in the trunk of the politician's car, death threats sending legislators into permanent exile, underage hookers working out of state property, broken arms and emergency dental work in the wee hours of the night. None of which anyone in Connecticut knew about, including me.

"Of course, I'd deny under oath any of that happened," he said. "But still, good prep for my current career."

His suit was well tailored, molded to his slim, fit form. He sat comfortably in his chair, legs crossed, the drink in one hand, the other dangling from the armrest. Olivia, in contrast, sat ramrod straight, a look of amused calm frozen on her face. She avoided looking at me, staying fixed on him. I tried to send her a telepathic message to loosen up, to act as if this encounter was the most natural thing in the world. She didn't hear it.

"Well, really, Erik this is quite a surprise. I wish you'd told me you were coming down here. You could have joined us for dinner. We've already had enough shop talk."

"I might have been interested," he said, then held up his hand. "Not about any confidential stuff, just about what exactly a management consultant does."

"We look at a client's watch and tell him what time it is," I said.

He smiled at that.

"I knew it."

"The truth behind the joke is that my clients usually have most of the solutions to their problems sitting before them. I like to say that objectivity is worth sixty IQ points. I might go out and buy a new sports car, and you'd be thinking, man, this dude really needs an SUV. Even the highly self-aware can't know things about themselves that are readily apparent to everyone else."

He listened carefully to what I said, concentrating. At least that was my conclusion, though I had to accept that the novelty of those icy blue eyes interfered with the signals. Too much of a distraction, too other worldly.

He looked over at Olivia when he said, "That is freaking interesting. I do a lot of the same thing in my own gig, intuitively, but I never heard it talked about that way."

"I imagine intuition played a big role in your police work," I said. "Especially undercover, where a single slipup could cost you your life."

"You imagine correctly," he said. "The trick was to be smarter than all those other guys, some of them wicked smart, but make them think you were dumber than a rock."

Pride of accomplishment slipped out of his fortress demeanor. Out of Olivia as well, by association, since she'd doubtless heard plenty of his stories of derring-do. Their eyes linked in appreciation of the moment.

"I don't know how you guys do it," I said. "Dealing with life and death the way people like me deal with inventory shortages and currency fluctuations."

He reluctantly broke eye contact with Olivia, who gave her head a little shake, as if casting off a spell.

"Everybody's got their part to play," he said. "Anyway, I should let you two finish up your business." He stood up more abruptly than social convention allowed. "I'm heading back to the hotel. I didn't check in since you're already there," he said to Olivia.

"You know which hotel?" she asked, her voice flat and dim.

His expression said, "Of course."

"Come find me in the bar." He stuck out his hand. "Nice meeting you, Dr. Waters. Good luck with the job. In fact, good luck with everything. It's the one thing none of us can afford to lose."

I shook his hand and watched him leave the restaurant. The expelled air from Olivia could have inflated the Goodyear blimp. At the end of the breath she said, "Fuck."

I didn't respond, using that precious moment to commit observation to memory, an effort undermined by Olivia repeating the same word over and over.

"What now?" I asked her.

"I'm wondering how to get my passport out of the house and make it back down to JFK so I can fly to a remote location and never come back."

If fear was a physical force, the waves emanating from her body would have blown the restaurant patrons out on the sidewalk.

"He knows," I said.

"He does. I'm so stupid to think I could hide anything from him."

I asked her a question I'd never asked before.

"Why so afraid?"

She gripped my forearm, digging in her long nails.

"You have no idea."

She jumped out of her chair, took a quick sip of water, kissed me on the cheek, and said, "I'm sorry. Please stay away."

She walked out of the restaurant with far less casual ease than Erik with a K. I looked around and none of the other customers seemed to take any notice, floating in their own bubbles.

Disappointment flooded my mind. Emptiness filled the restaurant, and the street outside, and all of Midtown Manhattan. I took the napkin off my lap, folded it into a diamond shape, and placed it gently on the table. The waiter approached, and I handed him my credit card, asking that he add 20 percent to the tab.

Back on the street, I searched out another hotel, where I checked in, dashing to a little shop in the lobby in time to buy a toothbrush and toothpaste, a shaving kit, and a T-shirt that declared the wearer loved New York.

The next morning, I retrieved my duffel bag and laptop from my room at Olivia's hotel, and caught the next train out of Grand Central to New Haven. I had plenty of seating options in the barely filled train, and selected one that made it easy to slide down with my legs extended and close my eyes so I could pretend to sleep. I quieted my mind by trying to wipe it clean of all thought. I was so successful at this that a conductor had to wake me up when we reached New Haven, the train's final destination.

"Sorry to disturb you, man, but it's the last stop," she said. "I hope you weren't supposed to get off somewhere back there." Once I got my bearings, I assured her I was in the right place. She watched while I collected my stuff and prepared to get off the train. "I was sorry to wake you," she said, with a bright smile. "You was so peaceful looking. You okay to get home?"

The kindness writ across her face was almost unbearable. I wanted to put my hand on her arm and express gratitude, but instead simply clasped my hands and bowed my head, and said, "Thank you. You're a good person."

I rode the Harley back to my motel, faster than I should have, and drank a beer while splayed on the top of the bed, where I fought off a militia of angry demons before forcing myself out of bed and back out into the world.

The next day, I logged on to ChatJazz, which had a message from Plato posted three days earlier.

"Revenge is an act of passion; vengeance of justice. Injuries are revenged; crimes are avenged."

Finally something we could agree on, I thought, before clicking out of the website.

CHAPTER THIRTEEN

J oey Adams was waiting for me when I got to the office.

"Megan wants to see you," he said.

"Know what it's about?"

"Official or unofficial?"

"Both. In order."

"Officially, it's a routine catchup. On the other hand, Megan was holed up in the main conference room all day yesterday with two guys in plain grey suits and boring ties, guys I'd never seen before. She had me bring in lunch from the cafeteria. They turned over papers that were out on the table when I came in to take their orders. Didn't say please or thank you. Who doesn't say please or thank you?"

"How did Megan look?"

"Like the whitest white girl in America. Even her freckles were white. At least she was polite. When the dudes left, she disappeared into her office and is still there. Her admin spent half the night bringing her files. Something's cooking, chief, that's for sure."

I thanked him and walked through the administrative area to Megan's corner lair. The door was locked, but she let me in after I told her it was me. Normally an orderly person, her desk and conference table were covered in piles of paper, and Bankers Boxes were stacked all over the floor.

She was wearing yoga pants and had her hair pulled back in a ponytail.

She just said, "Sit."

She joined me at the conference table.

"You know the temperature regulators we've been supplying to the air force?" she asked.

I said, of course, given that winning the contract a few years before had been a transforming achievement for the company.

"Do you know about the five-year procurement audits?" she asked. I did. They were a big deal, far more comprehensive than the standard annual review, absorbing big chunks of time from employees throughout the organization, as well as outside suppliers. We'd just gone through it a few months before.

"Great," she said. "Now, what about the penalty for defrauding the US government. Are you current on that?"

"No. But I suppose it depends on the size and nature of the fraud."

"How about fucking big, and flagrantly illegal?" There was no answer for that one. So I sat quietly and watched her squeeze her eyes tight and clench her hands in her lap. "It's bad, Waters. It's really, really bad."

I remembered a professor back at Penn insisting that we post-graduate psychology students learn important semantic distinctions, among which was fear versus horror. He said fear was a barking dog rushing at you from a dark alley. Horror was contemplating the Zombie apocalypse. One an immediate, focused reaction, the other a wider appreciation of a systemic terror that was poised to overwhelm everything.

What flowed from Megan was horror. She was throttled by a vast complex of interwoven fears. What made it even more horrible, was how it came out of nowhere, a jolt of exploding nerves, a hound of the Baskervilles that would rend your flesh into molecules.

I rolled my chair over to where she sat and took her right hand in both of mine.

"First, the job of those auditors is to create as much dread as they possibly can, to flood your nervous system with fight/flight hormones that undermine your ability to think. Scare you into abject surrender. Second, a lot can happen between a failed audit and a final ruling. This is just the opening shot. A time to stand up and fight, not curl up in a ball."

She looked down at the floor and nodded her head.

"I like what you just said, but I'm not sure how much more of this I can take."

"A lot more than you think. And you're not alone. I'm with you no matter what. I can't speak for Warner and Colin Brice, but I bet they'll stick with you too. Megan, look at me." I used the tips of my fingers to lift her chin. "You're a tough girl, surrounded by tough guys who believe in you."

I meant everything I said, even as I wondered if Frank Capra could have written better lines.

"I wish you weren't gay," she said. "Because I know what I'd want to be doing with you right now."

"I'm not gay," I said.

"You're not? What about Joey?"

"You people don't actually think that, do you? That's a real insult to him. He's got a husband and three kids. I've never met a more devoted family man. Or a better man, period."

She did another scrunching thing with her eyes.

"I'm sorry, Waters. God, I'm all fucked up."

"That's okay. You've got good reasons. Who else knows about this?"

"Nobody. I've been pulling all the records and reports I'm aware of. Eventually I'm going to need Warner and Colin to fill in the gaps. They've got to be brought in to this anyway. It's not fair to keep them in the dark. Even if those slimy procurement auditors told me to keep it on a need-to-know basis. Personally, I need to know how to shove knitting needles up their asses."

Megan had grown up in a poor Irish neighborhood in Brooklyn, and when tensions rose, I could hear her native accent creep into her speech. On that day, whatever affectations she'd acquired had vanished.

"I agree. Bring Warner and Brice in right away," I said. "We'll take this on together. They're good men. And no way could they have been involved. Brice is fairly new and Warner was always out of the finance loop. And anyway, he's Warner."

The implication being if Warner was crooked, nothing on earth would ever make sense again.

Megan's shoulders eased a little, and her harried breathing slowed.

"Oh God, Waters. I'm so frightened."

"Have you slept?"

"No. I was up all night pulling these files."

"Go home," I said. "Take a bath, have a glass or two of wine, and go to bed. When you wake up, the nightmare will still be here, but you'll be better equipped to handle it."

She nodded, probably entranced with the suggestion, permission of sorts to let it go for at least a brief time.

"You're gonna be around for a while, aren't you, Waters? I need you here. I can't do this on my own."

I assured her I was in for the duration.

"That's good news," she said, her head bobbing forward, some measure of solace forcing her toward collapse. I took out my phone and called Joey Adams, letting her hear me ask if he could drive her home.

He said, "Absolutely. Be right there."

She slid off her chair and curled into a ball on the floor, in direct defiance of my advice. I lay down next to her and stroked her hair, kinky and slightly greasy, and not exactly smelling fresh from the beauty parlor.

"Sorry about the gay thing," she said, her face buried in the crook of her arm, muffling her voice. "Not that there's anything wrong with it. You're single, but never hit on any of the women here. Including me, despite my best efforts. You come alone to the Christmas party. You clean up really well and you're built like a brick shit house. What the hell are we supposed to think?"

"Stereotypes can be useful, but often misleading," I said.

She sighed, as if settling into her exhausted surrender.

"Sometimes I wonder if you were manufactured somewhere. Is there such a thing as a scientific thug? Like the Terminator with an advanced degree. But I like you anyway. Can't explain it."

"I like you, too, Megan. I've been programmed to like intelligent women who hide behind the artifice of helpless naïveté."

She wiggled her butt into the front of my pants.

"We both have our secrets," she said.

I was able to get us off the floor and reasonably straightened up in time for Joey to arrive with a set of keys in his hand and a worried look on his face. I told him she'd been up all night and needed to get home as soon as possible.

He offered his hand, but she waved him away, thanking him for his concern. She walked out of the office on her own steam, while Joey hovered protectively. I was left behind with all the boxes and piles of records and reports, inside of which was either catastrophe or redemption. There was no way to know how long it would take to discover which it would be. Or how much of this was connected to the other calamities recently delivered upon the firm. And me. But it was my bet that the connection was absolute. I added another quality to the killer's profile: patient.

Back in my office, I did something I'd never done before. I looked up Olivia Lefèvre on LinkedIn. Her photo gave me a jolt, so beautiful and professional at the same time. Two qualities of great advantage in the business of executive recruitment. Her résumé was equally impressive, some of which I knew, and it was no surprise she'd gone to Saint Bridget's in Brooklyn, a Catholic school for gifted girls.

She listed her current employer as Reece & Reece Recruiters, Branford, CT. I called them, asking to be put through to Ms. Lefèvre.

"She's not available, sir, would you like her voice mail?"

"I understand she's actually taken a leave of absence," I said.

There was a long silence.

"We're not in a position to share that type of information, sir. Do you want her voice mail?"

"Sure."

Hearing her recorded message gave me another jolt. The sound of her voice freighted with an encyclopedia of complex emotions.

"Hey, Olivia. I'm keenly interested in making contact. I want to know how you're faring, and there is much to tell you. A response in any form would be much appreciated."

I ended the call and sat still in my seat, composing myself, wondering for the millionth time if anxiety had to be such a constant presence. My heart rate had increased, and my mouth was strangely dry. My mind, habitually filled with intricate strategies, was focused solely on a single desire— that Olivia would give me a phone call. It was sad to think she wouldn't, that I would never hear from her again. The last time I felt that type of sadness was when I asked my brother why I hadn't seen our dog for a few days, and he told me she'd been killed by a car.

I knew the clinical definition of anxiety: distress or uneasiness of mind caused by the fear of danger or misfortune, real or imagined. But now I thought they'd left out another form of wretchedness, a type of grief that was both felt and anticipated.

It wasn't until late in the afternoon that we finally convened a meeting with Megan, Brice, Warner, and myself. Megan looked like she'd almost pulled herself together and her voice was steady as she laid out the situation.

I knew enough about ExciteAble operations to do my job training and motivating its employees and counseling management, but it was a broad, general knowledge. It didn't take much to get lost in the details. I'd have sessions with Paresh where I'd learn just enough to keep up with the conversation, and an hour after leaving the meeting it would all go poof.

While Megan's description of the problem covered familiar territory for Brice and Warner, I strained to keep up. I was astonished at how much she knew about our technology, customer contracts, and financial arrangements. I decided I'd have to have one of them give me a dumbed-down version later on. Though I took one stab at summarizing the situation we'd found ourselves in.

"So you're saying, Megan, that the records say we overcharged the government on a big contract and they caught us in the five-year audit, triggering automatic litigation under something called the Federal False Claims Act."

"That's basically it," said Brice finally. "Not good."

"Not good?" said Megan, her voice rising a notch. "You can look up the penalties. Based on the alleged dollar amount of the fraud, without factoring in other civil fines that could be layered on, it's a death sentence. The end of ExciteAble. And personal bankruptcy for moi."

"What about liability insurance?" asked Brice.

"Doesn't cover illegal behavior," I said, as we finally had a subject I knew something about. "We'd have to prove we're just screw-ups, not criminals. With a government penalty, that can be a pretty fine distinction. Our insurance carrier has roomfuls of lawyers who know how to draw that line."

The room went silent for a few moments, as the state of affairs settled in.

"How did they catch us in the audit?" asked Brice.

"That's for them to know and us to find out," said Megan.

"We can't force them?" I asked.

"Not until we go to court," she said. "We can't wait for that. Most of the information we need should be in those files"—she waved her hand over the stacks on the conference table—"but I'm not sure. I'll need your help while I plow through it all."

A new thought leaped into my mind.

"*Qui tam*," I said.

"*Qu'est-ce que c'est?*" Megan asked.

"Whistleblower. They might know because somebody told them."

Another blanket of silence descended on the room, this one filled with even more dread. We all looked at each other.

"I'm operating on the assumption that it's nobody in this room," said Megan, "but I will handle the inquiry personally.

Your jobs are to trust each other and keep this place going. I know you can do that."

"We will," said Warner. "Just tell us what you need."

"Absolutely," said Brice.

I would have joined in, but another thought, given birth by the prior Gestalt, arrived in my head. It was a BGO, what another of my grad school professors called a Blinding Glimpse of the Obvious.

"Yolanda Alexander," I said.

"She of the bad handwriting and catty tongue?" Brice asked.

The former ExciteAble CFO was the type of employee pop psychologists call a Saboteur, characterized by sycophantic behavior with superiors while spreading malicious gossip, and committing vicious, sub-rosa attacks on the lower ranks. I didn't want to hire her in the first place; it was one of the few times Paresh overruled me. It took me a few months to figure out why I had that bad feeling, and about a month after that to put together documentation to prove I was right. But then she beat me to it and quit.

She obviously had the motive and the means to doctor both my personal accounts, and the billing process. She competed in triathlons and wouldn't need much of a handicap to match me in the weight room. And then there was the mechanical voice on the other end of the phone lines.

Was our boy a girl?

I noticed that I was parked next to Colin Brice in the company parking lot immediately before I saw him heading toward his car. He was in his usual sports coat and tie, a deviation from ExciteAble's unofficial dress code, though understandable for a financial guy who cleaved to the broader traditions of his profession.

I waited till he got there so I could ask him a question.

"Say, Colin, any idea why your employee file isn't with HR like the rest of us?"

He pushed a button on his key fob and I heard the doors of his car unlock.

"Do you want the polite answer, or the not so polite," he said.

"The most honest."

"My file is none of your goddamned business. We can work together, but I see no reason to give up my personal privacy. And I like you, but I don't know what you're really up to."

"I'm trying to keep this company going."

"Good to hear," he said. He got into his car and rolled down the window. "Megan can try to compel me, but if she does, I'll quit." His face suddenly shone with a familiar, albeit incongruous smile. "And then both of you can kiss my ass."

With that, he rolled up the window and slid his expensive imported car out of the parking lot, leaving me in the wake of a deeper understanding of our chief financial officer.

——— • ———

A ROUGH count of the Yolanda Alexanders in the country, based on Google, social media sites, and other available records, was about three thousand. Another five hundred were up in Canada.

I knew it would take Shapiro about five seconds to track her down using her social security number, which I had. But I was torn. I wanted to be a good partner to him, and an eager sharer, if only to reinforce that I was an innocent party. And I liked him. I didn't want him to dislike me, which would cut me off from the rapport we'd developed.

On the other hand, I craved independence, control over what I did and how I did it. I'd spent a lifetime doing things differently from everyone else, sometimes to good effect, other times disastrous. But this was who I was. It was impossible to change that.

I sat there in my desolate motel room and asked my brother, through telepathy, what to do. He said track down Yolanda on my own, since she was ostensibly involved in a matter outside the murder of Paresh and my own persecution. This DOD fraud was an entirely different issue, not included in my deal with Shapiro. The detective would never buy that argument, of course, but you can't have everything.

I stumbled around the Internet in my amateur style and found a website that promised to quickly track people down based on a minimum of information. I took them up on it, and it did narrow the search to about two hundred Yolandas. None listed ExciteAble as a former employer. So I jumped back to social media, and eliminated another large batch based on their photos. The twelve remaining Yolandas hadn't posted their portraits. Based on a few shreds of differentiation, I was able to cross out three of them by searching Google images.

Nine were left. Of these, five lived in New England, though only one in Connecticut. She was in West Hartford, so I drove up there and knocked on her door. An overweight woman opened the door. Not my Yolanda Alexander. She looked a little frightened, which was understandable. I apologized, said I had the wrong address, and left without another word. As with my conversation with the carpenter in New Britain, the moment left me feeling foolish and callow. But from those feelings sprung an idea.

I called my lawyer, Jadeen Knox.

"Long time no hear," she said. "The cops comin' after you again?"

"I don't think so. I just have a question for you."

"Fire away."

"I'm trying to locate our former CFO. We've uncovered issues in the financial accounting and need her to clarify. But the contact info we have on her goes nowhere, and I can't find her through the Internet. I'm close, I think, with eight good candidates, but I can't pin her down. We have her social security number, but you can't search by that on the people finder sites I'm using."

"I don't hold much stock in those online services. My PIs subscribe to much more serious firepower," she said. "I can ask."

"I'd appreciate it."

"Just takes money. My boys are good, but they aren't cheap."

"Isn't that what they say about you?"

"Known by the company you keep, Dr. Waters."

I gave her the stats on Yolanda that I was working with, including her social security number, prior work experience, and education, to pass along to the detectives, then went back to the motel.

Meager as my computer skills were, I thought I could at least do a Google search of my own.

It's often the most obvious things one can overlook, proven by a news article dated the month prior, that I found after about ten minutes of searching:

"Yolanda Alexander, Financial Consultant,
    Dies in Mountain Bike Accident."

Chapter Fourteen

It takes about three hours to drive from New Haven to Bennington, Vermont. The obituary reported that Yolanda had been visiting her sister, an economics professor at Bennington College, when she'd gone out for a morning ride along a demanding bike trail, and had apparently lost control along a narrow passage, causing her to fly into a ravine and smash into a pile of rocks.

I'd debated calling her sister, Belinda, before driving all the way up there, but decided the chances she'd talk to me were better if I just showed up rather than contact her by other means. This approach hadn't always worked out, but I wasn't yet ready to give it up.

It was early Friday and I was in a rented compact SUV, not feeling prepared for a six-hour round trip on a motorcycle, even one as sturdy and manageable as the Harley Sportster. The threat of rain was a deciding factor.

Bennington was tucked into the southwest corner of Vermont, where the air was clear, and wealthy transplants, rural poverty, progressive politics, and colonial history all coexisted, though how easily it was hard to tell from inside the little SUV. I had looked up Professor Alexander's schedule at the college, so I timed my arrival with enough leeway to catch her emerging from her ten o'clock class.

I had her official college portrait on my smartphone, and she looked enough like Yolanda to confirm the ID. Even more so in person, though her wardrobe contrasted dramatically with Yolanda's. A ripped sweatshirt, leggings, and a short denim skirt in lieu of grey and black suits, high-top Converse sneakers instead of sensible flats.

"Belinda Alexander?"

She didn't seem disturbed at all to be approached.

"You bet. What's up?"

"I'm from ExciteAble Technologies. Your sister, Yolanda, worked for us. I'm sorry for your loss."

She looked both curious and annoyed.

"Me too. No more Alexanders from this line. What can I do for you?"

"I'd like to ask you some things about Yolanda."

"What kind of things?" she asked.

"It's pretty complicated. Can we sit down somewhere?"

She started walking and I followed her. We went down a long hall, then through a door that led to an open space, dotted with park benches. She took the one farthest from the door.

She sat down and pulled a bagel from her giant handbag.

"I always sit here after my Friday class," she said. "Room for two on the bench," she added, tapping the seat next to her.

She started to break off pieces of the bagel and toss them on the ground. In short order several squirrels ran up and snatched their share of the prize.

"Squirrels are much smarter than people realize," she said. "And cuter. Just look at those little hands. So what about Yolanda?"

"I don't mean to speak ill of the dead, but I think she was manipulating my company's financial records."

"You just spoke ill of the dead."

I pointed to one of the squirrels.

"He's getting most of the bagel. But he's skinnier than the others."

"More athletic. Will live longer," she said.

The sun was hot on my face, and the bench oddly comfortable. I slid down and rested my head.

"You don't have to talk to me if you don't want to," I said. "But if you're okay with it, I'd like to ask some fairly difficult questions."

I kept my eyes on the squirrels, but I could see Belinda studying me, literally sizing me up.

"How well did you know her?" she asked.

"Not very. Though enough to have her fired if she hadn't quit first."

I immediately regretted saying that. Candor is compelling but can be premature when you know so little about the person you're speaking with.

"How long did it take you?" she asked.

"About six months."

"That was faster than most. Now that she's gone, I'm the last one standing. Everyone else is gone. I have no significant other, no children, no nieces or nephews. There might be a cousin in California, but I think she's a family myth. I'm basically alone."

"I figured that," I said.

"Google?"

I closed my eyes.

"Just a guess."

"What did you say you did for your company?"

"I'm an organizational psychologist. I focus on human resources, training, and counseling senior management."

"I could have guessed that too. Do you want to take a ride?"

"Sure."

She stood up and stalked across the grass. I followed. We passed students and older adults, faculty and staff. Only a few said hello. The trek took about twenty minutes, ending at a parking lot, where we climbed into an ancient Subaru Outback with a five-speed manual transmission. It was clean and well-maintained, the boxes and file folders filling the back seat neatly stacked. The front passenger seat was empty, so she didn't have to clear a spot for me. When she turned on the engine, Green Day blasted out of the speakers. She snapped off the stereo.

An artfully contrived representation of a piano keyboard was pasted on the dash. It was worn in places, suggesting heavy use.

I caressed it, and she said, "Sometimes I like to play along."

I'd only been to Vermont a few times, and was taken by all the open space, big mounds of green hills and squalid, rusted car-strewn hovels interspersed among pretty little clusters of buildings and majestic, ancient homes. And cows. And forlorn attempts at roadside enterprise. Healthy-looking young people on racing bikes sharing the road with pickups the states to the south would condemn as lethal hazards. I guessed it was like any other place. A mixed bag. Just with nicer air and a sense of freedom the congested regions of New England wouldn't understand.

Belinda said I seemed comfortable not conversing, even trapped inside the confines of a small car with a person I'd just met. I told her that was true, though I could talk about a variety of subjects if she wished. She said she was fine with silence. It allowed her to concentrate on holding the Subaru

straight on the road, imbalanced as it was by the unaccustomed bulk in the passenger seat.

At one point she reached over and felt my shoulder
and left breast, noting that muscle was much heavier than
fat, which explained why a man of my average height and
girth was causing the car to list so far to starboard. She said
Yolanda had the same effect, though less so. She said her
sister was the fitness freak of the two siblings, while Belinda
held up the sedentary, uncoordinated department. She did
earn a letter in high school for winning the state chess cham-
pionship, though technically chess wasn't a sport at all.

It became obvious that my reticence actually provided
plenty of dead air for her to gladly fill. She told me she and
Yolanda had been raised by their father after their mother
abandoned them, taking off in the middle of the night with
a carpenter she'd met in the midst of renovating the family
home her father had inherited from a bachelor uncle. It was
in Silver Springs, Maryland, and their father taught mari-
time law at Georgetown University's Walsh School of Foreign Service.

The father chain-smoked and probably would have lost
his untenured position over poor hygiene if Belinda hadn't
been relentless with his laundry and insistence that he take
a shower at least every two days. At the end of the month,
she rubbed antiseptic cream on his nose to reduce a chronic,
mysterious redness, and dragged him to the barber, who
plucked hairs from his ears and attempted to tame his dis-
reputable beard.

Unlike most of her colleagues, she loved her students'
idealism, which she described as hopelessly delusional, especially as it related to economics, her chosen field. She felt her
mission was to prepare them as gently as possible for entry
into real life, which she characterized as a pitiless urban

wasteland, red in tooth and claw. Or maybe just a comfortable existence within desolate suburbia. The few who had escaped, usually to tropical third world cesspools of pestilence, anarchy, and death, likely had a lot more fun, short-lived though it would turn out to be.

"On the other hand," she said, "most of them still send me Christmas cards. And seem to be breeding and caring for fluffy cats and Labrador retrievers."

After about a half hour, we turned onto a narrow, lumpy macadam road, which soon devolved into gravel, then rutted dirt, narrowing enough to force us between branches swatting at the Subaru from both sides. People's houses, intermittently placed, fell away, giving up to tangled foliage and rotting stumps, and felled trunks pushed clear by unknown forces.

She seemed confident in the road ahead, often gunning the Subaru over seemingly impassible swampy patches and through leafy tunnels clogged with branches that hung like lazy impediments across the passageway. I gripped the handhold to avoid knocking into her. None of this turbulence interfered with her monologue.

She was fairly certain her father had begun having sex with Yolanda when her sister reached puberty, though could never quite prove it. Yolanda's preference for sheer nightgowns at the dinner table, unabashed masturbation on the toilet seat in their shared bathroom, and constant tiptoeing around the house late at night was solid evidence, but not probative.

She and Yolanda had one thing in common, an exceptional facility with mathematics. The older of the two, she often wondered if Yolanda might have taken a different path if Belinda hadn't been there to compete with. Music, perhaps, which she said was structurally a form of math, unless you're talking about atonal, arrhythmic, experimental things that nobody listened to anyway. Yolanda had taught herself viola, which seemed to correlate with less bedwetting, though when she gave that up, she started cutting her thighs and forearms with razor blades.

A habit that ended when Yolanda turned thirteen and became obsessed with Federico Fellini, which led to teaching herself Italian so she could appreciate his movies in their original language. An unfortunate side effect of this enthusiasm was a shift from Fellini to Mario Puzo, and subsequently the *Godfather* movies, which further transferred to an infatuation with actual gangsters, the old-fashioned Sicilian variety. Living in Silver Springs, there wasn't a lot of organized crime within easy driving distance (if you don't count the federal government), so she had to travel north to Baltimore, where a regional franchise of the Gambino family maintained a lively little business.

The result was a string of black-haired young men wearing Members Only jackets and large gold rings rotating through the household, whom Belinda remembered as being rather sweet and polite to her father, addressing him as Professor Alexander and showing amazement that a single person could own more books than the whole library in their neighborhood. Not that they ever went into their libraries.

This phase ended when the Maryland State Police showed up at the house one night, late, with a search warrant, leading to the discovery of a .25 caliber semiautomatic Saturday Night Special that ballistics proved was used to put a bullet into the head of a man alleged to have insulted the girlfriend of the owner of the gun. Subsequent legal proceedings established that the suspect, one of Yolanda's boyfriends, had a rock-solid alibi, leading investigators to briefly turn their suspicions on the girlfriend herself, Yolanda.

The case eventually fizzled out, through lack of evidence, and Belinda gratefully returned to her college studies, having been Yolanda's principal support, since their father claimed an overwhelming workload, what with grading term papers and overstuffed class schedules, and private tutoring.

Yolanda also refocused on academics and managed to graduate from high school with a good enough average to get into Princeton, where she made it through sophomore year before dropping out and completing her degree at Rutgers, the graduating school she listed on her application to ExciteAble Technologies.

Belinda was happy enough that things seemed to turn out all right for her sister during this period, and never asked how she'd been able to pay her own way through college, or where the Cadillac SUV had come from.

It wasn't the first time that mysterious objects had shown up in Yolanda's possession, beginning at around age five, with a hamster, which Yolanda cared for with fanatical devotion, and articles of clothing that Belinda knew her father would never have known how to purchase.

A fire at the house belonging to the parents of a girl who had scratched Yolanda's face on the school bus had also stirred Belinda's suspicions, but as with other incidents, proof was elusive.

After college their shared enthusiasm for math diverted into separate career paths, with Belinda working her way through her master's and PhD in economics and Yolanda getting her CPA, before sliding into one of the giant accounting firms headquartered in New York City. Contact between the two became less frequent. This meant that Belinda was unaware of her sister's peripatetic journey through the accounting profession, logging brief stints at a dozen firms before going client-side, positions secured through the use of increasingly mythical résumés and strategically chosen references.

She apologized for her dim view of the screening process managed by recruiters and HR departments, and I said she didn't have to. We're not all that careful, and in our defense, employment law provided plenty of refuge for candidates with Yolanda's serial violations.

My ears had popped twice before we reached a clearing on the crest of the hill we'd been climbing. Before us was a vast expanse of lumpy, dark green terrain, interrupted here and there by open fields of lighter green and gold. She said on a clear day you could see Albany, New York, to the right, Williamstown, Massachusetts, to the left. She walked to the mouth of a trail, and I followed her. It was more difficult for her to keep up her soliloquy, being forced to turn back toward me so I could hear her, but she only confirmed what I already knew—that Yolanda needed hard, nearly continuous exercise in order to function. She had to keep moving like a shark, she added, with a crooked grin.

About a half hour into the trail, we stopped on a narrow ridge, with precipitous drops to either side.

"Is this where it happened?" I asked.

"No," she said. "Let's keep walking a little farther."

Minutes later, the topography changed again, with the ground rising slightly to the left, and to the right a six-foot-wide strip of wild grass, which provided a border between the trail and another steep cliff. She held me from behind by the shoulders and walked me over to a spot where the grass was torn up, close enough to the edge of the precipice to see down into a rocky ravine. She pointed at the grass.

"See that gouge, and another scrape over there," she said. "Now, look to the left at the woods. This is where she went down, and then over. What do you think happened?"

I assumed it wasn't the obvious, but I said it anyway to get to her point.

"Her bike fell to the right, causing the gouges, and she rolled over and off the cliff."

"Yolanda had ridden that mountain bike the equivalent of here to the moon," said Belinda. "Only fell twice badly enough to require medical help. You saw that section of trail back there, a lot more treacherous than this. But that's not why I wanted you to see it." She was looking into the woods. Thick enough to hide a person.

"She was pushed," I said.

CHAPTER FIFTEEN

I could easily see it. Yolanda is speeding along, her eyes fixed on the trail, mindful of the hazard to the right. Someone lurches out from behind the big hardwood trees to the left and gives her a shove. The bike hits the ground hard. Either she goes right over, or is kicked, shoved, or dragged the rest of the way. For at least thirty feet, it's a straight drop into a jumble of sharp-edged rocks. If Belinda hadn't called the rangers to say her sister had failed to come home from her ride, Yolanda would probably still be down there, likely dismembered by predators and scavenging birds.

"What did the cops say?"

"They didn't agree. Declared it an accident. To be fair to them, the forest rangers got here first, and tromped all over the site. Then it rained for a full day before I convinced the Bennington PD to take a look. Still," she added, her voice trailing off.

The walk back to the car was a sad, quiet trip. She let me go first, and it seemed to go more quickly than the walk to the site. When we were back in the car, I asked her about Yolanda's love life.

She said it paralleled her work life. Numerous, diverse, and short-lived. It wasn't a common topic of conversation, so Belinda imagined it was worse than she knew. Dates and lovers included men and women, in a range of ages, along with their socioeconomic standings. Belinda never bothered to retain much in the way of specifics, knowing they would likely change in short order, and not knowing how much of it was actually true. Yolanda had always lied as effortlessly as she breathed, for no particular benefit, often distorting the facts in a way that cast a poor light on herself. Whatever she was saying at the time was her reality, fact and fiction entirely fungible and of equivalent value.

"What about the funeral? Did you capture any names or contact information?"

"That'd be easy, since I was the only one there," she said, "except for the funeral parlor guys and this religious dude. Funny, really."

"Why?"

"We're atheists, but the funeral guys talked me into letting a Unitarian minister come by and say a few words before we tossed her ashes into the lake behind my house. Just in case, they said, and I was amused enough to go along. Before he left, I told him, with all due respect, that we should hope for Yolanda's sake that there's no heaven or hell."

I knew what she was going to say next, so I filled it in.

"Because you knew which direction she'd be heading."

Jadeen Knox seemed almost glad to see me when she came out to the reception area. I followed her to her sumptuous office where we sat next to each other on a leather couch.

"I used a news article to locate Yolanda's sister, Belinda, whom she was visiting up in Vermont where the accident happened," I said. "Though Belinda and I are convinced it wasn't an accident."

"Say what?"

"How much time do you have?"

She had enough that I was able to give her a fairly comprehensive rundown, leaving out what I considered irrelevant biographical details, except to note that I had a lot of them. An expert listener, she stayed fixed on my eyes as I spoke, as if they provided a direct link from the testimony to her memory banks.

I asked her what more the detectives she referred me to might be able to learn.

"Social security number is the key to the realm," she said. "With that they can learn a whole lot more. Prior employment, addresses, credit history, criminal record, pretty much the whole shootin' match. Now, she might've stolen other numbers, which is not beyond the possible, given her wiles, and need to cover her tracks. You're not thinkin' she's your killer, are you?"

"I was hoping, but unless she knows how to reach out from the grave, the timing's off. But an accomplice? Absolutely."

"Talk to them directly," she said. "Otherwise, you'll be paying me and paying them. If the cops decide to reactivate your case and I'm still your counsel, we'll discuss how we go forward."

"Thank you. That's very generous of you."

She scoffed at that.

"Not like I got nothing else going on. Just do me a favor and get Shapiro back in the loop as soon as possible. You get that crafty bastard's nose out of joint and I'll be back on your payroll in a New York second."

"Understood."

The next few days I was buried in work, much of which I slashed down to the manageable with the valiant assistance of Joey Adams. Friday afternoon, when everyone else had bolted for the weekend, we were sitting in my office organizing the next wave of assignments.

"What's your job title?" I asked him.

Though likely surprised I didn't know, he said, "Employee Development Coordinator."

"You're now Employee Development Manager. Forty percent raise. Make your own decisions when I'm not here. I'll support them all. If you screw up, you'll have learned a valuable lesson. Send me written plans and program schedules to revise if necessary and approve. Save the sensitive stuff for when we can speak face-to-face. I'll be in as much as possible, but I've got a situation here, as you know, and I don't want important projects to lag because I'm not always available. I trust you and respect your judgment and sensibilities. I need your help and you deserve the opportunity."

He looked a little like he'd just seen a flying saucer land in the parking lot.

"Geez, boss. That's a lot to take in."

"You got all weekend to talk it over with your husband before texting me to say yes and we'll sort out the details Monday morning."

"I don't need to discuss it. I'm in."

"Okay. And the fucking up part? Try not to do it."

"Got it."

On the way out, I cleared Joey's promotion with Megan, who acted like it was such a good idea I didn't need to clear it, though we both knew I did. I asked her how things were going with the False Claims case and Sarnac and his offer to buy the company. She said tense. On the plus side, Brice and Warner were acting like The Greatest Heroes of the Western World, working like animals to strengthen the core of the operation and maintain profitability, while spending countless late hours investigating the fraud itself—how it happened, who did it, how deep it ran, what other booby traps were waiting to blow up.

"I'm not disappearing, Megan, but I need some chunks of time off," I told her. "Joey's got our department under control, Brice and Warner are holding up their end, and you can always call me, and I'll be here before you can hang up the phone."

"That's an exaggeration, but I get the idea."

She looked pretty good. Shoulders straight, no bags under her eyes, steady hands, and a strong set to her jaw. Just some new crow's feet etched in her delicate Irish skin. Sloppy casual clothes, sneakers, and hoodie instead of high heels and pinched skirt. No makeup. Ready for a rumble.

"Until we learn who killed Paresh, nothing can work, and none of us are safe," I said. "You know that, don't you?" She nodded her head. "I like the New Haven detective on the case, but his time and resources are limited. So I'm going to hire private investigators to help with this. I'll need the company to pick up the tab."

She said of course.

"What a screwed-up world we got here, don't we," she said.

"You're a brave person."

"For a woman?"

"I don't distinguish between the genders when it comes to courage and moral rectitude," I said.

Her eyes started to fill with tears, but she willed herself to make them stop. Maybe because I'd told her to never let anyone see her cry.

"Who taught you that lesson?" she asked.

"My brother."

"Maybe we should get him working on this situation."

"We can't," I said.

"How come?"

"He's dead."

They called their detective agency Los Umbros. There were two of them, Billy and Glen, and as Jadeen reported, they were indeed boyish and very big.

Billy's wife provided administrative help. She greeted me at the front desk and alerted the team by yelling over the cubicles behind her. They emerged at the same time, as if choreographed. Both wore blazers over tieless shirts, but were distinguishable by hair color: one blond, one black, both buzz cuts.

We went into a third cubicle, which had a round table and credenza, where a coffee maker and a plate full of donuts awaited. Billy's wife followed with some paperwork attached to a clipboard, explaining I only had to fill them out if I became a client.

Proof of their certifications hung on the cubicle walls, along with a calendar, a few kids' drawings and two newspaper clippings, one reporting the recovery of an eight-year-old girl whose father had fled with her to Thailand in the midst of a custody battle, the other about tracking down a tractor trailer filled with prescription painkillers boosted from a warehouse in New Jersey.

Billy, seeing me looking at the articles, said, "Kids to eighteen-wheelers. We do 'em all."

I told them the referral from attorney Knox was good enough for me.

"She's a pisser, that Jadeen," said Glen. "You probably don't know she used to be on the job."

"A cop," said Billy. "Like us. Surprised the shit out of us when she gets into Yale. Rides it all the way through law school."

"So what can we do you out of?" Glen asked.

"You know about the murder of Paresh Rajput, CEO of ExciteAble Technologies?" I asked.

"Yeah, we figured you for that one," said Billy.

"Let's start with I didn't do it," I said. "And go from there."

The story took about an hour to get through, mostly because they often stopped me to ask questions. In doing so, they betrayed an unexpected knowledge of things like aerospace technology, closely held corporations, and generally accepted accounting principles. As well as more expected, like cyber security and labor laws.

"So," said Billy, "where do we come in?"

"Background checks on our employees. HR uses an online service, but you know how superficial they can be. I want to go deeper. Without going crazy overall. I want the crazy effort on Yolanda Alexander."

"As in full personal and employment history, to see if you can connect the dots between her and the unknown perpetrator of the homicide, attempted framing of yourself—for that murder and various financial offenses—not to mention the stalking and threats, and the guy sent to kick your ass," said Billy. "I can see why all this would be of interest to you."

Glen thought that was amusing.

"Don't forget the possible murder of Yolanda herself, the Federal False Claims charge, and the fact that somebody's been stealing toilet paper out of the utility closet," I said.

Glen liked that even more. I set a manila envelope down on the table and put a flash drive next to the envelope.

"You'll see instructions on accessing employee records. If you need other information, let me know and I'll make the arrangements. Somebody purged Yolanda's employee file, which was probably full of bullshit anyway. But I do have all her e-mails, including the ones sent to us from her personal address when we were recruiting her. Also on the flash drive is a description of our CFO, Colin Brice. I don't have his file either, which is troublesome. Anything there would be good to know."

"So I guess that means we're hired," said Glen, sliding the clipboard in front of me.

In the mood for detectives, I drove my Harley over to Westbrook, about a half hour from New Haven, where Erik with a K shared a coastal home with Olivia Lefèvre. The house was bigger than its neighbors', with more lawn to buffer the congestion that lined the shore. According to his website, Erik ran his PI business out of that house. A full-sized, late-model Jaguar was in the driveway. Olivia drove an Audi SUV, which wasn't there.

A parking lot serving the beach was about a hundred yards past the house. I pulled the Harley up close to the public bathrooms and walked back down the block. I referred to my smartphone to confirm I had the right house. There was a front door, and another on the side along the driveway. No signs directing potential customers, so I went up to the front door and rang the doorbell.

Erik was schooled in hiding his reactions, but surprise still shot across his face, then just as quickly, disappeared.

"You remember me?" I asked.

"Not sure. Have we met?"

"In New York. I was having dinner with Olivia. You treated her with an unexpected appearance."

"Oh, yeah. The VP of operations. What can I do for you?"

"I didn't take the job, just so you know. The CEO turned out to be a dick. But I remembered you were a private investigator, and I really could use one about now."

"Most people call ahead."

"I was in the neighborhood and remembered you and Olivia had a place here. I took a chance."

He paused for a moment, then stood back to give me room to enter the house. The living room looked and smelled like a well-maintained bed-and-breakfast. Old furniture, polished and nicely preserved. Early twentieth-century rattan living room set with cushions covered in bright, floral fabric. A model of a three-masted schooner over the fireplace.

Erik wore a black T-shirt that exposed arms with stringy, veined muscles. He offered me a seat. Then he asked for me to wait while he went upstairs, saying it would only be a moment. I said of course.

"What kind of trouble you got?" he asked when he came back, pulling up a straight-backed chair, easier to get out of than the low-slung rattan.

"Business trouble. Some rich bastard is trying to buy the company I work for, which is why I was looking to get out, but now I think it'd be better to stay put. Which leaves the matter of the rich bastard. He's getting cozy with the founder's widow, who's got the mental capacity of a June bug. And the majority of the stock. Me and the other management staff would love to break up that little love fest."

While listening, Erik's face showed no affect, and he'd kept both feet flat on the floor and his hands resting on his thighs, fingers spread. His eyes never left my face. In his tight T-shirt and jeans, the only place to store a gun was in an ankle holster. But then, if it were me, I'd have my legs crossed for quicker access. I felt my own little semiautomatic pressed against my back.

"Sounds interesting, but I'm a little busy at the moment."

"The guy's offering a big payout, and terrific synergies, which we know means bringing in his own people to run the place," I said. "Our combined salaries are a little north of a million dollars, and we control the corporate budget. Could include a line item for the services of an outside security specialist. A big one."

His face soured, but that signaled serious evaluation, not annoyance. He relaxed slightly, though kept his posture on alert.

"So what do you want from me?" he asked.

"Everything you can learn about this guy's personal and professional life. Anything that would be compromising enough to make him pull the offer," I said. "I assume that's within your skill set."

The suggestion of insult caused the slightest tic in his expression, immediately checked.

"It is," he said. "Only question is why pick me?"

"You're Olivia's significant other. I trust her completely. What other qualifications do I need?"

A certain level of wariness would be expected in a PI being interviewed for an assignment like this, but Erik's went deeper than that. Complex calculations flickered behind his fixed gaze.

"And I pay cash," I said, pulling a roll of hundred-dollar bills tied by a rubber band from my pocket. I tossed it a little high and to the right. He caught it with his left hand, without looking, reflexes like a busy terrier.

While he counted the money, I wrote down Nelson Sarnac's name and address, and the website of his holding company, on the back of my business card. I handed it to him when I got up to leave.

"Do you have a card?" I asked.

He dug one out of his wallet.

"How's Olivia doing, by the way?" I asked, as I went through the door, pausing on the stoop. "I keep trying to reach her, but no response. I still might need another job if this whole thing blows up."

"She's taking some time off to be with her mother," he said. "Old broad is about to cash in her chips."

"Sorry about that. Extend my sympathies if you will. And by the way, you're a lucky man."

"How's that?"

"She's the most beautiful woman I've ever worked with. With brains to match. Rare as hen's teeth."

His control began to waver, but he pulled it back.

"I wouldn't know about that," he said.

"Fair enough. Just tell her I hope to hear from her as soon as it's convenient. We have a lot of catching up to do."

"I'm sure you do," he said, as he softly closed the door in my face.

Sitting on the Harley, I used my smartphone to go on a genealogy website and search for Olivia and her family. I found her mother's name, and did another search, which linked to a site called tombstones.com. There she was, buried in another Connecticut shoreline town, next to her husband, Olivia's father. I expanded the photo so I could read the words chiseled into the stone.

"A Unique Mother."

And the date of her death, ten years before.

CHAPTER SIXTEEN

I had dinner with Noah Shapiro that night. I told him he was way too sophisticated a cop to bribe with a simple box of donuts. Instead, we had a table at the old Union League on the New Haven Green. The Beaux Arts interior and French cuisine provided an ambience in keeping with the high level of corruption I was contemplating.

"Nice place," he said. "My father eats here every Thursday night. Gets the early bird Kosher bouillabaisse. We're not Kosher, before you ask. And you and I are splittin' the tab. Can't accept gifts."

"That's a relief," I said.

They put us by the window and fluttered around the table, pouring water and taking drink orders and clearing unneeded set-ups. Shapiro didn't look at the menu, claiming he knew it well.

"Sometimes I drop in to hang with Pops," he said. "A chance to catch up with family news and get a good meal in the bargain. And he likes the company, even though he won't admit it. Especially since my mom died."

I waited until we were engaged with our meals to get to the point of the evening.

"I decided I'm going about this in the wrong way," I said.

"How so?"

I first put him through a brief survey of the current literature on managing obsessive, malignant narcissists, citing the relevant journals and commentators. They usually relished lots of interaction, allowing them to feast on attention, and manipulate the object of their obsession into greater and greater involvement. So the usual prescription was to make the victim unavailable. Cut off all contact, if possible. Evade all attempts to engage, which is what I'd been doing. With some success, I thought, having forced him into communicating through the chat site. But that was too impersonal, too anonymous, since it left fewer ways to terrorize me. It had been several days since he'd made contact of any sort, which was disturbing.

"Why?" Shapiro asked.

"He's been on what experts on stalkers and obsessive revenge-seekers call a 'pathway to violence.' It's a step-by-step process, gradually escalating. By choking off the opportunities for regular, relatively small doses of harassment, I'm forcing him to jump a few steps, which could lead to a grandstand play. Something big to match his frustration and growing neediness."

"Something like offing your ass," he said.

"Yes. And that would be an unfortunate thing. Your odds of catching him will drop to near zero."

"Seems pretty counterintuitive. By keeping yourself safe, you're actually increasing the odds this nutbag will take you out of the game."

"That's right," I said. "I need to go the other way. Make myself as available as possible. Give him a target-rich environment. By increasing contact, we improve the likelihood he'll expose himself, hand us a channel we can follow back to the source."

"You want to be bait."

"Draw out the enemy. A strategy as old as Sun Tzu."

Shapiro thought that over for a while.

"You're a free agent, Dr. Waters. You can do what you want. But it's unethical of me to condone it."

"Though you will try to keep me alive," I said.

"I will."

I asked him if the FBI had made any progress tracing back Plato's posts. He nodded.

"Sorry, forgot to tell you that they originate in Connecticut, but via stolen wireless access. Three different locations, about as far apart as possible and still be in our little state."

He told me they'd also started the process of getting full access to Plato's ChatJazz account, which could lead to identifying the actual user, and his full correspondence.

"Though don't hold your breath," he said. "These things can take a long time. Privacy, protected speech, First Amendment, blah-blah-blah. All things I believe in, by the way, except when I'm trying to lock up a murderer."

I told him about the last posting, reciting the quote.

"Samuel Johnson," he said, "and his contrasting definitions of vengeance and revenge. Splitting hairs in my mind, and a distinction without a difference in the eyes of the law."

"It's what forced me to reevaluate my strategy," I said. "It taught me something about the killer. I believed from the beginning that he was driven by a sense of self-righteous revenge. This quote and the handle he picked for himself, Plato, confirm that."

"Plato?"

"The first philosopher to lay down the fundamental principles of justice," I said. "The killer knows his stuff. But more importantly, he's aligning himself with the greatest historical thinkers. Rich narcissist ego food. As satisfying as this meal in front of me."

I spent the rest of the night briefing him on my visit with Belinda Alexander, and the reason for it. He agreed Yolanda was an excellent lead, making a strong prima facie case for her as an accomplice, and he liked that I'd hired Los Umbros to gather up information on her past associations. Especially since it wouldn't come out of his departmental budget.

"It's these sorts of public-private partnerships that forge strong bonds within our community," he said.

"You got my vote, Shapiro."

The next day I checked out of the motel and drove my Harley to the condo, which the cops had released to me a few weeks before. Even outside the door, the smell was palpable. Inside, much worse. The whole place was covered in multicolored fingerprint powder and the wall-to-wall carpet looked like Jackson Pollack had been trapped there for a few days with a case of booze and a box full of paints.

I called commercial cleaning services until I found one that promised to be there the next day. Then I left for the office, wondering if I'd ever be able to reinhabit the place, and if not, how I'd be able to sell it.

I checked into ExciteAble, and thankfully, there were no pressing demands. Megan, Brice, and Warner had set up a windowless war room secured by industrial-strength padlocks and security cams. They were all in there, methodically poring over spreadsheets and reports. Joey told me Megan put out an office e-mail saying we were working on a big new contract, an exciting prospect, so for everyone to do their bit and keep production going while management focused on the opportunity. He thought they bought the explanation, though personally, he didn't.

"You're going to let me know what's really going on when you can, right, chief?"

"Just keep pulling the oars, Joey. I'll watch your back."

"Ditto. The training schedules you asked me for are in your e-mail. *Répondez vous*, ASAP, if you don't mind."

"Will do."

I left to go east to Branford, where I dropped in on Reece & Reece Recruiters. They were in a small office building made to look like a big colonial house, with a nice view of the harbor. The receptionist was a young man with a beard that almost disguised an operation correcting his cleft palate. His speech was only slightly impaired.

"Miss Lefèvre is out of the office, sir. Do you want to leave a message?"

"I know she's out. I'm hoping you have a phone number or a forwarding address."

"We aren't in a position to share that information, sir."

"*You* may not be, but maybe somebody else is." He spoke his unease with his whole body. "See if you can roust her boss. I guarantee he or she will want to at least talk with me. I'll be waiting over there."

Then I turned around and made myself comfortable on one of the waiting room's luxuriant couches. I wondered if the hopes and desperation of waiting applicants had seeped into the leather upholstery.

A stern man appeared in the waiting area. He wore a white shirt and unimaginative tie, but no suit jacket. His hair was grey and his jaw set in the locked-down position. Despite the imperious deportment, I figured he was less than forty-five years old. He looked at me in an assertive way likely practiced over a lifetime.

He said he was Joel Reece. I said nice to meet you, not volunteering my own name. He led me into a conference room.

"You were asking for Olivia Lefèvre," he said. "And I think you've been told she's unavailable."

I wasn't ready with a good reason for Olivia's company to disclose her whereabouts, knowing that no reason would ever be good enough. Withholding from me wasn't only easy, it was the most legally and morally prudent thing to do. So I took another approach.

"I've been told. They also said I could leave a message. I'll take that option." He checked his watch, expressing that I'd just wasted some of his precious time. "But I have to know it got to her, and not lost in the company e-mail system," I said, regaining his attention.

"We have other very able recruiters you could work with," he said. "I could transfer the relationship immediately."

"It's not business," I said. "It's personal."

He blanched.

"That's not my department," he said.

I remembered the lesson the carpenter in New Britain had given me, that false pretenses were the weakest of strategies. Thus, the truth was almost always the strongest. I moved closer to him, making him aware that this time his hyper-masculinity would not be an advantage.

"Her life is in grave danger."

His head lurched back, alarmed. And something else, a trace of fear. As if a pin had punctured his outer shell and all the dominance was escaping into the air.

"I don't understand," he said, meaning he did understand, but was hoping he was wrong.

"I'm just asking you to send her a message. A text to her cell phone will do. If you don't, it will make you complicit in her death," I said. Then very quietly, voice pitched to the lower register. "And I will hold you personally responsible."

I moved even closer, well past the boundaries of his personal space. The remaining color left his face. He took a step back, and I followed him.

"Do you have identification?" he asked.

"You don't want to know who I am. You don't ever want to see me again. And you won't, as soon as you send her that text." I pointed to the smartphone hanging on his belt. "Do it now. I don't have time to fool around."

"You're threatening me," he said, looking over my shoulder at the door.

I lowered my voice to a near whisper.

"No, I'm not. I'm telling you that if you don't do that one simple thing, and anything happens to Olivia, I will be back, and you won't like it."

His cognitive dissonance was loud enough to hear through his skull. He was unused to being challenged on any level, and never so directly. And like all bullies, he was unaccustomed to fear, and thus more susceptible to its effects.

I watched him pull the phone out of the holster as if the act was beyond his will. He swiped and pecked around for a moment.

"What's the message?" he asked.

"Okay or not okay," I said. "With a question mark."

He tapped it in, then showed me the little screen where the text appeared as sent.

"Satisfied?"

I grabbed the phone. He tried to resist, but I twisted it out of his hand. Then I selected the number he used and forwarded it to my own phone. He looked betrayed, and furious. Though still diminished.

"I hope that text wasn't sent to your dry cleaners," I said, tossing his phone on the conference room table.

"I gave her a chance when no one else would," he said. "I thought that would mean something to people like you."

"People like who?"

His face closed down, a form of stress-related paralysis I'd seen before. Usually when confusion was stirred into fear and loathing. It meant his value to me was all used up, so I left.

The receptionist stared at me as I crossed the waiting area. I stopped and stared back until he averted his eyes.

———— • ————

I HAD to spend two more nights in a hotel while they finished cleaning up my condo, only this time I went upscale. Big fluffy beds, thick walls, coffee maker and plenty of water pressure. I used my regular credit card and signed on to the hotel's wireless.

I sent an e-mail to the people I worked with to announce my imminent return home. I went back to the gym, and as with my prior hiatus, did stretches for half an hour, then light weights for a half hour after that. My spotting partner showed no curiosity over my absence, and I showed no interest in her.

I renewed my regular shopping and restaurant habits. I retrieved my car from long-term parking at the airport, and after moving back into the condo, parked it in my assigned spot. My only concession to modest security was keeping the Harley inside the condo, with no objections from the neighbors, who as a rule abided by a live-and-let-live philosophy.

The cleaners had done a good job. Everything was gleaming, and the evil smells were bleached into submission. I didn't have much in the way of furniture and decoration to put back in place, but it was satisfying to do so. I took some modest precautions: A locksmith installed heavy-duty deadbolts on all the doors. A security company put in motion detectors wired to a burglar alarm, and placed an invisible camera in the outside hall, with discreet monitors in the bedroom, living room, and kitchen. All tied to an app on my smartphone, which would alert me if an intruder came in while I was away.

My handgun was either on my person or tucked under my pillow when I slept. I bought a pair of pump-action, 12-gauge shotguns, putting one in the hall closet and the other under the sofa in the living room.

Home is where the heavy artillery is.

———— • ————

THEN A message came from Olivia.

"Am alive. Please don't call. Miss you."

I read the text a few dozen times, trying to glean secret messages that clearly weren't there. I used the text as a mantra when I worked out, and a way to help me go to sleep at night, abbreviating it to simply, "Am alive. Miss you."

Having made a habit of riding the Harley, I rarely used my car, though whenever I did, I always checked for GPS trackers. It was a time-consuming task, but one evening, while running my hand along the undercarriage, I felt a little plastic box.

I left it where it was and started to use the car for routine errands around town. On one of these, I noticed a Dodge Charger had followed me through two turns. It was a few cars back and seemed to be matching my speed as I went through a series of lights along a busy stretch of retail.

It was starting to get dark as I drove northeast into a less congested residential area. The Dodge had to work at keeping other cars between us, but I made it as easy as possible. By the time we reached a road that went through open countryside, the Dodge was right behind me.

Night had mostly settled, and the headlights from the Dodge crept closer. I checked the GPS on my phone, and a few miles later, made a strategic turn onto a long, nearly empty stretch of road that ran through a big dairy farm.

By now, the Dodge was tailgating me, its lights filling my rearview mirror. I started to slow down, keeping a firm grip on the steering wheel. I could hear the other car's engine, a high-performance rumble that got louder as the slowing speed forced it to downshift. As we approached an area with open land to the right, I cocked the wheel slightly in that direction, laid back against the headrest, and hit the brakes.

The impact threw my car off the road, lifting it up on two wheels and spinning it into the opposite direction. The car rocked to a stop and I jumped out. I stood behind the open driver's side door. The Dodge made a hard-right turn and drove off the road, roaring back toward me.

Two guys got out of the Dodge. Each held a baseball bat. I pulled the automatic out of my rear waistband, and using the open window as support, shot out their headlights. They froze in place.

"Toss the bats and lie facedown," I yelled.

The driver complied. The other one said, "Fuck you."

I shot him in the leg. So now he was down as well, though faceup, clutching his thigh and screaming obscenities. I walked over to him and kicked the bat out of his reach. My eyes were still adjusting to the ambient light, but I could make out his face.

Mike Wojcik.

I pointed the gun at his midsection.

"This gun is unregistered," I said. "There's nobody around, and no way to connect me with killing both of you. Tell me why I shouldn't do it."

"It's murder," he said.

"It's self-defense. Though I'll never have to face a jury."

"Don't fucking do it," said the other guy. "I'll do anything you want."

"Who sent you?" I asked, pointing the gun over in his direction.

"Ask Wojcik," he said. "He knows."

"Fuck you," said Wojcik. I swung the gun back and fired two rounds, one to either side of his head. "The guy," he yelled, "he sent me another grand. I never seen him."

"Bullshit," said his partner.

"Don't say anything," said Wojcik.

"If you don't tell me anything," I said, "I have no reason to keep you alive."

"Tell him, you moron," said the partner.

"I need a doctor," said Wojcik. "I'm bleeding to death."

"Good. It'll save a bullet." I looked over at his partner. "Come on, get up, let's take a ride."

But before he could, Wojcik said, "I'm in front of my house about to get out of the truck when the guy pulls up, wearing this stupid Homer Simpson mask. I told him I didn't want to work for him anymore. He tells me to take the job or he'll kill me and my whole family. And all of my friends. He drops an envelope on the ground and takes off. It's full of cash with a note about what I'm supposed to do."

"Give it to me," I said, reaching out my hand.

"Come on," he said.

"You can keep the money. I want the note and the envelope."

He said it was in his back pocket. I made him roll over, and I took it out. In so doing, I saw an exit wound on the back of his thigh. He rolled back, groaning and cursing. I found the note and took out the money and dropped it on the ground. I went over to his partner and had him stand with his hands in the air. I searched him from behind and found his phone. No gun. I made him get back on the ground. Then I went to the trunk of my car and pulled out a coil of clothesline. I tossed it over to the partner and told him to make a tourniquet for Wojcik's leg and get him to the nearest hospital as soon as I drove away.

"You might as well let me bleed out," said Wojcik. "Homer's gonna get me anyway."

"Maybe. I'd have your family leave town and join them as soon as you're out of the hospital. I haven't met him, but I don't think it's worth his time and effort to chase you down, much less kill you all."

I didn't know that for sure, but I thought I was right. As I made my way back to the condo, I concentrated on how to keep the killer busy enough to take his mind off this latest failure, and his wrath diverted from Mike Wojcik.

To see if I could turn myself into even tastier bait.

CHAPTER SEVENTEEN

I looked up the hospital closest to where I shot Mike Wojcik. It was a good distance from New Haven, well out of Shapiro's jurisdiction. I waited a few days, then called the hospital pretending to be a Medicaid claims adjuster. I didn't know if there was such a thing, but the nurse on the trauma floor confirmed without hesitation that she had a patient named Michael Wojcik and that he'd be released the next day.

I waited another few days, then drove over to New Britain and rang his doorbell. No answer. And no vehicles either in the driveway or the garage. I called his cell and got a recording that said if the call regarded the business, to please contact so and so at so and so number. All other calls, please leave a message and he'd get back to you as soon as he could.

Hoping the dope and his family were safe, I moved on to another concern—what to tell Shapiro. I wanted to throw the envelope and instruction note into the evidence pile, but I didn't know how to explain where it came from. I thought it was unlikely the killer had left DNA or prints behind, but not inconceivable. But there were too many risks in the real story, even if fudged or partially told. Shapiro was too smart to buy any bullshit. And even if he let me off the hook for all the felonies associated with the gun, there was no way he'd let me keep it.

I'd just have to see if an answer would come to me.

Meanwhile, I could read the note, which I did at the condo. I wore surgical gloves and held the small card by the edges.

The instructions were printed on the card. They directed Wojcik to go to a shopping plaza near my condo at six P.M. and await further direction. If no word came by eight, to go home and repeat the same thing the next evening. He could expect something to happen within a few days. At that time, he'd be guided to a moving car, which he was to follow. Additional instructions would be provided at that time, but to be prepared with a baseball bat.

I often described The Great Escape, the survival game I played, as four-dimensional chess. You had to move within reality's three dimensions, but also plan those moves within the fourth dimension, time. Not only did circumstances change over time, but each stage in the process had to be considered as a set of future potentials, and contingencies readied for each. You could never fully achieve this, since the if/thens quickly branched toward an infinite number, but any effort working out possible, contrasting scenarios was worth it.

The killer would be a formidable competitor if he knew how to run, swim, crawl through the mud and underbrush, and come up with a better disguise than Homer Simpson.

Erik with a K called to say he wanted to meet. He had some preliminary thoughts about how to proceed with the investigation of Nelson Sarnac and wanted to show me something before moving forward. I said sure, and he gave me an address of a coffee shop in the town of Woodbridge, right outside New London, Connecticut.

"We'll take it from there," he said.

I called my other PI service, Los Umbros, to see how they were coming with their project. I got the two of them on conference call.

"Moving along," said Billy. "Like you thought, that girl had a whole lot more going on than she wrote on her résumé. Amazing, really, how you can jump from job to job and nobody knows anything about it."

"Let me know when you're three-quarters done. No e-mail, just give me a call."

"Got it."

"What about Colin Brice?" I asked.

"I started looking, but not a lot of success. You'd be surprised how many Colin Brices there are out there. But I can refocus on him."

"No. Stick with Yolanda. Meanwhile, there's someone else I want to add to the list."

"Name it," said Billy.

"You know a PI named Erik Humboldt?"

"Of course," he said, after a pause. "We know every PI in the state, at least by name."

"How about reputation?"

He paused again. Even without a visual, I knew he was being circumspect, picking his words carefully.

"He left NYPD after getting cleared in a deadly force hearing. Dead guy was a Wall Streeter, not your usual wasted fool or kid with a toy gun. Or some innocent dude just taking a ride with his girlfriend. This one stumbled into Humboldt's undercover work on a two-grand-a-night call girl operation. Apparently, while Humboldt was listening on a wire placed in this guy's apartment, the guy starts getting a little rough with one of the ladies. Humboldt makes a hard call and busts in. Allegedly panicked, the guy pulls a gun. Humboldt takes issue with this and drills the guy through the head.

Responding officer secures the scene minutes later, CSIs and the ME confirm it's a clean shooting, zip-zip."

Glen came on.

"Next thing we know, he's up here working our turf. No big deal. Plenty of room for everybody. We just asked around the NYPD anyway, evaluating the competition. Officially, his people closed ranks. Unofficially, there's some head scratching. For some reason, Humboldt killed the wire before running into the apartment to save the day, so there's no audio. And based on the time the audio ended, and Humboldt's call to report the incident, it's about a half hour. The deadly force review board didn't seem to care about that, but curious minds wondered otherwise."

"Humboldt hadn't made a lot of friends," said Billy. "A loner. No law against it. What I noticed was they all seemed a little intimidated by the guy. Not a common thing among cops."

"How about looking at him a little closer," I said. "Any ethical issues with that?"

"Hell no. We'll look at anybody," said Glen. "The only person I'm intimidated by is my mother-in-law."

"Rightly so," I told him, and got off the line.

I drove my car out to Woodbridge, which was a straight shot down I-95, a highway notorious for chewing up motorcycles. The coffee shop was less than a mile in from the exit, and Erik was waiting for me at a table that faced the door, and within a few steps of the emergency exit.

He watched me get a cup for myself, ignoring the tablet device in front of him.

"I drink it black," he said, as I sat my cup on the table. "Putting lots of crap in coffee is an abomination, in my opinion."

"I favor a tablespoon of light cream. No more, no less."

"Your Nelson Sarnac is an interesting cat," he said, sitting back in his seat.

"I agree."

He pointed at his tablet.

"I've been chasing him around on this thing all week," he said.

"What happened to old-fashioned shoe leather?"

"Went out with neoprene soles. The only thing you wear out now is the tip of your finger. I could do it all on my computer at the house, but I like to get out and around. Hang in places like this. Who do you think owns it?"

"Nelson Sarnac?"

He grinned in a way I'd rarely seen. Lots of teeth, curled upper lip, not unlike Humphrey Bogart.

"Depends on how you look at it, is the honest answer," he said. "Let's take a ride."

We walked out to his Jaguar. As soon as the doors were closed, all sound from the outside ceased. He pushed a button, and the engine started, though barely detectable. I loved the feeling of being free of external stimuli.

He pulled out of the lot and headed south toward the interstate, which we drove under and continued on to the coast of Long Island Sound. It was an industrial park, with low-slung, flat-roofed buildings and fleets of commercial vans and utility trucks in the parking lots. Sea gulls flew overhead.

He told me we weren't far from Millstone, a nuclear power plant. The businesses we were driving by had sprung up all around the area as soon as the plant reached critical mass.

We crested a small hill, and the sound was suddenly there before us, a blue-grey expanse beyond which you could see nearby Fishers Island, a low strip of green interrupted by the occasional stately home. Lighthouses warned of navigational hazards and boats moved silently over the surface of the water.

The road ended at the pebble beach, blocked off by a permanent metal barrier. To our right was typical scrub land, tangled foliage eking out an existence on the nutrient-poor sandy soil. To the left was a tall, two-hundred-foot-long display case. The sculpture within was a tightly woven, neatly composed maze of pipes and pressure vessels, of seemingly random diameter, painted a brilliant assortment of reds, oranges, yellow, and silver.

"What is it?" I asked.

"A natural gas distribution center. The contractor who built it also did all the plumbing at Millstone. They thought it was so beautiful they put in the glass wall, on their own nickel. Hardly anyone knows it's here. If I was Woodbridge I'd be charging admission, but with Millstone next door, they aren't keen on people hanging around this part of the shore."

According to Erik, John D. Rockefeller was the richest man in American history, by a healthy margin. He did it not by producing oil, but transporting it from the wells to his refineries, and then on to the factories and power plants.

"Like my old man used to tell me, there's a lot of money in plumbing."

"Sarnac," I said.

"One of his offshore companies has a 51 percent stake in that thing, just enough to maintain control. It's fully automated, needing only a maintenance contract with a local company that checks on the control systems and makes sure nothing's leaking. The closest you can get to owning a money machine."

I'd assumed Erik would be spending his energies digging up embarrassing personal information on Sarnac. Illegitimate kids, scrapes with law enforcement, bad nights at the casino. I really didn't care, since my objective wasn't to compromise the hunted, but to get close to the hunter.

"Why hide your wealth?" I asked him.

"That's what I'm wondering."

"And if you're that rich, why mess around with a small aviation parts manufacturer?"

"I've seen enough to know people do shit all the time for surprising reasons," he said. "At this point, I'm not surprised by anything."

We agreed that pressing on with the investigation into Sarnac's business interests would be the most productive use of his time. I told him I admired what he'd already achieved, trying not to imply it was pretty sophisticated for a retired cop and one-man PI operation. As I said to Megan Rajput, stereotypes can be useful, but often misleading.

On the way back to my car, I resisted the temptation to ask after Olivia again. Nothing would be gained by showing too much interest, especially now that he was working for me. The truth is, I just wanted to talk about her with a common acquaintance, to hear her name spoken out loud and share in appreciation of her finer qualities.

An exceptionally irrational impulse, surprisingly difficult to suppress.

When I got back to the office, Megan was waiting for me, joined by Joey Adams. They were having coffee and feasting on a box of donut holes. She looked worn, but alert, as if a healthy version of her older self. Joey jumped up, suddenly feeling uncomfortable hanging around his boss's office with the CEO of the company. I told him to sit the hell back down, which he appreciated.

I let him linger through some small talk between us, before giving the signal to let Megan and me have the office to ourselves. He shut the door softly behind him.

She briefed me on the False Claims investigation. Our first assumptions were proving out. It was an act of sabotage, carried out at the financial management level. When Colin took them through the mechanics, he had to apologize a few times for admiring the perpetrator's cleverness. He said it reminded him of an embezzlement scheme they'd uncovered at his last employer's, where a schlub in accounts payable had skimmed off tiny amounts from thousands of transactions, but over time, accumulated significant dollars in separate bank accounts spread around the country. What he missed was a new algorithm the banks were using to report suspicious depositing behavior. Thus he was caught on the wrong side of the digital arms race, the global battle of machine versus machine.

I asked her if we could get Warner and Colin Brice to join the meeting, saying I had some information I should share with the group. While we were waiting, she asked me for a topline.

"Yolanda Alexander," I said.

They arrived at the same time and sat with us around the conference table. Colin popped a few donut holes into his mouth. Warner sat quietly, his thin limbs sticking out everywhere, like a long-legged bug.

I'd learned early on in my training exercises that people better absorbed information when delivered as a story, with a narrative arc. So it was important to put events in proper sequence, to build the climax on a solid foundation.

So I made them endure a brief description of antisocial personality disorder, a broad definition that manifests itself in a variety of ways. I bypassed the arguments over root causes, simply saying these people exist, how they got that way was irrelevant. I asked them to just accept the fact that we had one in our midst. And she was a doozy.

Megan looked horrified, Warner contemplative, Colin unfazed.

"The embezzler at my old company, he was one of those types," said Brice. "When we confronted him, he didn't react at all. No outrage, no defensiveness, no excuses. It was like we were talking about some other person in some other part of the company that had nothing to do with him. While we waited for the police to pick him up, we talked about the Patriots' prospects in the Super Bowl."

I had them picture Yolanda calmly working at her desk after hours, slipping in and out of the accounting system. Colin added what he'd said to me, that she didn't have to be a computer whiz to do the deed, just patient and careful in following direction, skills consummate in a financial person.

"It's doubtless that Yolanda was the one who shifted corporate funds into my private accounts, pinning the blame on Paresh," I said.

"Why?" asked Warner, despite my request to hold questions.

Unlike Colin's embezzler, the only thing she took out of the company was her salary. In other situations, I told them, I'd look for sabotage as an act of revenge, but she hadn't been at the company long enough to fight with management, or rack up grievances, aside from some petty squabbles with fellow employees. The day she quit we locked her out of all access to company computers.

"Consequently," I said, "the indisputable conclusion was she was working for someone else."

Like a secret operative dropped in behind enemy lines, sent in to perform certain defined tasks, for which she was paid a fee. We'd never know what other mischief she was going to do, and for how long, since she quit without warning, presumably mid-project.

"Yes, but why?" Warner repeated, his engineering mind seeking order and logic. "Why would someone hire Yolanda to do all this? What was their purpose?"

I let the question hang out there, to give space for my other colleagues. I was glad I did, because Megan had an answer.

"To destroy our company," she said. "That's what this is all about. Kill our founder and house genius. Ruin me emotionally in the process. Discredit his right arm, impute the integrity of our government contracts, sow discord and insecurity among the employees, generally fuck us to death."

Warner listened carefully, but his question still drifted above the conversation, unresolved. Out of kindness to Megan, he left it unsaid. I helped them both out.

"We don't know, Fred," I said. "We don't know why someone would want to do that. We only know he's succeeding."

Chapter Eighteen

While clearly not a dirt bike, the Harley Sportster was sturdy and agile, and had heavy springs and thick-walled tires. And the unpaved road was smooth and free of ruts and rocky hazards. It took me deep into a state park that my brother and I thought we owned growing up, since one of the most important trails started at the rear of our property, and in all the years we prowled over the terrain, we almost never saw another human being. Deer, fox, bear, coyote, rabbits in abundance, feral dogs and cats, snakes with potentially fatal venom, but few people, venomous or not.

As much as I relished the perception game, the absence of people whose faces, body language, and spoken words I obsessively interpreted, was a pleasing change of pace. For my brother, it was certainly a vast relief.

As if in response to the change in venue, even our conversations took a distinct path. I don't remember much of what I said, but he would often spend the entire time in the woods telling me stories that he made up as he went along. They were serialized, usually featuring two brothers who had created a time machine and had vivid adventures in the near and deep past, and into the future. They were nothing like the two of us. Both were geniuses, since who else could have built a time machine. The younger was the math specialist, who had spent weeks walking around the Princeton campus with Albert Einstein helping the old man work out the Grand Unification Theory. The elder was the master engineer, who could fabricate lasers out of old TV sets or rocket fuel from regular household cleaning products.

Scenes in the stories would often be inspired by creatures we came across—tadpoles becoming a swarm of flesh-eating lizards the size of our stepfather's Chevy Malibu. A diseased growth on the side of a tree would become a cosmic energy force that the big brother harnessed and placed at the center of a fusion reactor.

These were all my brother's creations. My contribution was to be the ideal audience, utterly absorbed and astonished at every invention of the mind.

Near the center of the park was a small community, abandoned in the early nineteenth century. The wooden structures were long gone, but the stone walls defining roads and fields, mortarless foundations with immense trees growing up through the middle, ancient cowbells and the rusted skeletons of buggies and wagons remained.

My brother told me that a kid in the town was captured by Indians who carried him off to the Great Plains where they hunted buffalo and lived in teepee cities that stretched to the horizon. One day he was watching Indian mothers planting potatoes and decided to help them. When he started digging, he didn't stop until he was in a hole over his head. That's when he knew what he had to do.

Escaping late at night, he walked all the way back to New England, and when he got to this little town, he yelled, "Hey, everybody, there's land out there with six feet of topsoil and not a tree or granite boulder to dig out of the ground. You best come and take a look."

I parked the Harley at the bottom of a steep incline and hiked up through the undergrowth to the familiar trail, where it spilled into a big stand of mature hemlocks, which shaded out all ground cover below, leaving a soft carpet of pine needles. The massive trunks of the hemlock trees were like the columns of a medieval cathedral, the canopy its roof, beneath which the sunless caverns wanted only for candles and chanting priests. The way through was printed on my memory, and I easily picked up the trail as it left the hemlock grove and meandered down the other side of the hill to the colonial ghost town.

I went to our favorite primeval foundation where we'd spend hours target practicing with a .22 rifle. I set up a row of small rocks, and standing at a modest distance, drew the automatic out of the holster at the small of my back and shot all but two of them into the air. Then I walked back twenty paces and blasted off the other two. I repeated this with another line of rocks, often shooting from a run or squatting position, from an increasing distance, until any successful hit was more luck than precision.

I went back to my original starting point, and went through the process again, until I nearly exhausted the ammunition in the clips stuffed into my pockets.

I heard my brother tell me I could shoot so well because I never let myself get in the way. Not that I was stupid, but I was so indifferent to hitting the target that I never choked or overthought the squeeze of the trigger. I didn't know what he meant at the time, but I believed him in this as in all other things.

I have little facility with numbers, but I'd looked at Olivia's phone number so many times it was fixed in my memory. The urge to call that number was nearly irresistible, and the fear of doing so overwhelming.

The main problem was lack of information. Her last call had been blocked, so I didn't know if it came from her own phone, tucked away in her purse, or someone else's, an imagined, malevolent figure waiting for her to unveil her subterfuge. I didn't know if the number Reece used to send the text was even hers. I didn't know if she would welcome the contact, despite her warning, or be enraged that I went against her wishes.

I didn't know anything. If she was safe or in great danger. Was she hoping I'd rescue her, or fearing I'd foolishly reveal her hiding spot?

A firm believer in collaboration, when faced with a difficult problem I'd normally seek advice. Two minds being better than one. Two or three more even better. But that was impossible. The most useful collaboration in this case would be with Detective Shapiro, who could probably work with the FBI to track her through her passport and credit cards. But I'd have to tell him why I wanted to find her, and that would open Pandora's box. A secret between two people was no longer a secret the moment it's learned by someone else. It surely couldn't be shared with the entire law enforcement community, foreign and domestic.

I couldn't even predict what my brother would say, though I thought he'd tilt toward doing as she asked. Stay away, which thus far I'd been doing. So maybe I was predicting after all.

CHAPTER NINETEEN

"I got an interesting call from the New Britain PD today," said Detective Shapiro, when I answered the phone. "They're holding a suspect in a larceny case who thinks he has something to trade. His name is Eddie Kozlowski. Know him?"

"You know I do," I said, reminding him of my story about tracking down Mike Wojcik.

"New Britain should give their sketch artist a raise. I got a picture here based on Kozlowski's description that looks exactly like you."

"So the thing he wants to trade has something to do with me," I said.

"Apparently. We're going up there later today to have a sit-down with Mr. Kozlowski. I'm guessing you want to come along."

"Name the time and place."

We met an officer in the lobby of the New Britain Police Department, a modern building in a developed part of the city. She wore a white shirt and Shapiro introduced her as the captain of the department. She led us through the bullet-proof glass door next to reception and into an interview room.

She told us Koz had been ratted out by a crew of burglars who'd been hitting the storerooms of big-box retailers up and down the local shopping strips. The detectives staged a meet and got him on tape with a trove of incriminating statements. When they played him the tape he said to call New Haven.

"Detective Shapiro told me you like to be in the room," she said to me. "Says you're experienced, and I trust his judgment. Just know it's not something we normally do with civilians. Safety concerns."

"Koz will be cuffed," said Shapiro.

"I've met him, Captain," I said. "Your concerns are warranted." Then I said to Shapiro, "Don't be fooled by his appearance. He's rightly touchy about it. We won't get him to talk if he feels disrespected."

They seemed to take that—and the suggestion that we be seated before he came in the room—without insult. The captain left us, and a few minutes later an officer brought him in, as promised in handcuffs and ill-fitting orange jumpsuit.

They'd given his hair and beard a jailhouse trim, which did little to alter the look of a malicious troll. He studied us, his face on the offense. When he sat, he put his cuffed hands on the table with a metallic clang, an awkward gesture given his height, but a signal that he was dangerous enough to warrant the precaution.

"Who's this joker?" he asked me, looking at Shapiro.

"Ask him yourself," I said.

He shrugged and looked around the room, as if not really caring to know.

"I'm the one who will decide the next ten or so years of your life," said Shapiro.

Silence gathered and slowly smothered the atmosphere. Kozlowski broke first, saying to Shapiro, "They told you I got some information you'll want to know?"

Shapiro let some more dead air accumulate, then said, "They told us. Worth a listen, coming from you."

The compliment, transparent as it was, seemed unexpected. Kozlowski settled more comfortably in his chair. He nodded toward me.

"He must've told you I got a bead on everything that goes on around here."

"He didn't have to. We knew that already," said Shapiro. "That doesn't exactly make you my favorite person. We got enough to do with all the boneheads doing stupid shit. A guy who can think just makes our lives harder."

It was remarkable how sweetly seductive flattery could be to those susceptible to its charms. Especially people who actually possessed some of the qualities that were being flattered. And had endured years of neglect, if not persecution, by lesser lights.

In some ways, I thought, this might be the greatest moment in Eddie Kozlowski's life.

"We've never seen anything like this heist concept you had with the big retailers," said Shapiro. "We don't expect you to tell us how you did it, but shit man, impressive. Though you'll appreciate that it's our job to put you away for a very long time, impressive or not."

Kozlowski wasn't as happy with that last bit. It was his chance to be as magnanimous as Shapiro, a test he flunked.

"I don't appreciate shit," he said.

Shapiro pretended to scratch his chin on his shoulder, giving us a second of eye contact. I darted my eyes toward the door, then back to Koz, who missed the exchange.

Shapiro looked at me and said, "I don't know about you, but I'm getting hungry. Great bar and grill across the street. I think happy hour starts in a few minutes."

He stood up to leave.

"Whoa, wait a minute," said Kozlowski. "I thought we were talking here."

Shapiro stuck his hands in his pockets.

"I was talking. You were hanging tough. I get it. That's your nature. But I got other things to do with my time."

I started getting up from my chair.

"You, sit the fuck down," Kozlowski said to me. "I haven't even told you what I have."

I paused, and Shapiro said, "Like, nothing?"

Kozlowski put his little hands in the air and wiggled them.

"What're you gonna give me?" he yelled. "We haven't even talked about that!"

Shapiro sat down again, directly across from Kozlowski, and said, in steady, quiet tones, "About ten years, best estimate. You'll love it up at Somers. Catch up on old times with guys from the neighborhood. You never fucked any of them over, did you, Koz? No, probably not. You're too smart for that."

I thought maybe Shapiro had pushed it too far. Kozlowski would have his share of enemies in prison, but probably a lot of friends as well. A man like him wouldn't have become a local deal maker without building loyalties and proving his worth as a source of reliable income. But I also knew he'd never done time, so he couldn't know for sure who would get to him first, friend or foe.

He set his eyes on me.

"You didn't come around my place for nothing," he said. "You want that guy bad. I seen it in your face. I've seen it before. A hunger. He wants him, too," he pointed at Shapiro, "but not as bad as you."

"That's why we're here," I said. "To find out what you know. I can't offer you any deals, but I will speak in your favor if you can help."

He looked over at the detective, skeptical. I didn't blame him. But I could sense him making a decision. He stared at my face, longer than necessary, I think to give the moment a cinematic feel.

"That envelope you dug out of my dumpster, that wasn't the only one. He sent me two. One for the instructions, then once I agreed, another for the money. This one he hand delivered. To my office."

He held his eyes on me, testing. I felt my pulse rise. It was a game called "I know something you don't, but you can figure it out if you try. If you're as good at the game as me."

His head was tilted toward the table, but he looked up at me sideways. A teasing look. The kind of gesture kids like, pretending to be deferential but really full of prideful mischief.

I heard Shapiro happily humming, as people do as a realization dawns.

"You saw him," I said.

"I did. He was wearing a Homer Simpson mask. So I didn't see his face. Unless it was actually Homer Simpson, though I'm doubting that."

"Good," said Shapiro. "He touch anything?"

"Wore gloves. Wouldn't sit down. Just handed me the money and told me he'd kill me and everyone I ever loved if I said anything about it."

"Describe what you did see. Race, color of hair, accent," said Shapiro.

"White guy with dark hair. No grey. No accent you'd notice, like New York or Boston. A little under six feet tall. Wore a long trench coat, but definitely not skinny or fat."

That was all he could remember, but it was a lot more than we had before. The Homer Simpson mask proved legitimacy. I was happy enough. I wasn't sure about the detective.

"That's good, Koz, but not exactly take-it-to-the-bank good," said Shapiro.

"I'm not even at the good part," he said, dragging the cuffs over the table so he could sit back.

"I suggest you tell us the good part without the preamble," I said. "My friend here has the patience of a five-year-old."

"Two," said Shapiro. "A two-year-old."

Kozlowski nodded, then bent into his story.

"Okay, we're done discussing our deal, and the guy holds his stomach, asking if I had a bathroom. I say sure, this is a fully equipped facility. He pulls a Glock out of that trench coat and points it at my head. Then he says, show me where it is. I take him there. It's got a single urinal and a toilet inside a stall, and you can lock the door. He makes me wait inside while he takes a dump. The stall's partway open, so he can see if I try to make a run for it. The poor bastard's got a mean case of the shits. You know what I mean. Fireworks going on in that stall."

Kozlowski grinned, and so did we. Relishing the discomfort of our shared enemy.

"When he's all done, we go back to my office," Koz went on, "and he leaves, after dishing out a few more threats. I say, yeah, yeah, fine, fine. Heard it all before. Soon as he's out the door, I head back to the bathroom with an empty coffee cup. I been complaining to the building owner for months about that toilet. You flush it, and you think it's all going down, but then some shit always floats back up into the bowl. Disgusting, really."

Shapiro barked out a little laugh.

"You have a piece of his shit," I said.

Kozlowski slapped his manacled hands on the table. "Bingo, baby. DNA."

Another hour was spent negotiating with Kozlowski, the captain, and the New Britain DA over what Koz got in return for handing over what we were then calling the sample. At the least, the DA said he could keep him out of the maximum-security prisons, away from former associates who might have long memories and short tempers. That was enough for Koz to tell us where he hid the cup.

Shapiro and I went and retrieved it, which Koz had stuck above the hanging ceiling in an empty office next door.

"Make sure you label that properly," I said. "One of your junior officers might think it's a latte."

On the way back to New Haven, hyped up over a possible breakthrough, Shapiro shared his philosophy on managing expectations.

"I expect the worst. Not just because I'm Jewish. I'm also experienced in the enchantments of disappointment, having been disappointed about a million times. You can't do this job if setbacks throw you. You have to look at each failure as an opportunity to set up the next success. Because success happens as well, just less frequently. So the trick is to produce as many setbacks as possible, increasing the odds that good things will appear. Like the lottery says, you can't win if you don't play."

I thought about that, appreciating the solid logic and wisdom in his words, before saying, "I don't expect."

"That's what I'm saying."

"No. You expect the worst," I said. "I just don't expect."

"That's not possible."

"For you."

"Tell me again what planet sent you here?"

"Planet Johnny and Evelyn Waters. You can blame it on them."

I met Megan Rajput at her house in a coastal Connecticut town near New Haven. It was a huge, rambling ranch house in a 1960s development of other ranches, same design obscured by decades of changing landscapes, renovations, and improvements. Comfortable, but the type of neighborhood people with a fraction of the Rajputs' income could easily afford.

She'd called me to set up a meeting when I was still in New Britain. Since it would take me a while to get there, she asked that I just come straight to her house.

She answered the door wearing a loose, floral thing, in bare feet, holding a big glass of red wine, claimed to be her first of the evening. I accepted a ginger ale on the rocks.

The inside of the house belied its plain exterior. Leather living room set, marble fireplace surround, subtle designer lighting, and artwork on pedestals and walls—a mix of Western and South Asian, including an ornate beast with its tongue hanging out and a ceramic elephant wearing a pair of yellow pants. Music came out of nowhere. A glass wall displayed a swimming pool, enclosed by stone work and more strategic lighting, red maples, and clouds of green foliage. That's where we headed, the night still warmed by the day, and plenty of lounging furniture to sit on.

I commented on the incongruities of her home—American middle class on the outside, *Architectural Digest* within.

"Paresh hated ostentation, I like decor. This was a compromise," she said. "He also thought conspicuous consumption attracted criminals. How ironic is that."

She propped her bare feet on a wicker ottoman and rubbed them together while taking a protracted sip of wine.

"I think ExciteAble's fucked," she said. "In layman's terms, totally fucked up the ass. That psycho-bitch Yolanda did a brilliant job doing false data entries in a way that made us all look guilty as hell. There's virtually no way of proving they weren't intended, since nothing came before, nothing to compare them to. Do you get what I mean?"

"I do. The incriminating evidence wasn't overlaid, it was primary. And linked to corporate officers, most importantly Paresh. Proves the power of an inside job. I'm sorry. I let you down."

She seemed startled by that.

"It's my job to prevent that exact thing from happening," I said. "I told Paresh not to hire her. He overruled me. I should have pushed back harder."

Megan shrugged it off.

"You're human. She was an expert bullshit artist. Don't beat yourself up."

"What does Nelson Sarnac think of all this?" I asked.

"He doesn't know."

"The chairman of the board doesn't know?"

"I don't have to tell him, legally, before the next board meeting, which is in about a month. As soon as I do, he'll be pushing the other board members to remove me, have lawyers swarming all over the place pestering my employees, doing all kinds of furious crap that'll tie up all my time. Can't deal with that right now."

She set her wine glass down on the slate patio and looked around at the cunningly beautiful surroundings. She wiggled in her seat, pulling down the hem of her dress, then thought better of it, and pulled it back up, showing a lot of pale, well-formed leg.

"I miss Paresh," she said. "I loved living in his life. With him gone, I don't know where I am."

I ignored that.

"Sarnac wants to buy your company. You might want him to, for your own sake, so maybe he should know what's what."

She retrieved the wine glass after some fumbling around and held it with two hands under her nose, as if a fine vintage deserving a sniff.

"You own the company, Megan. You can replace the whole board anytime you want, including Sarnac. Tell him about the False Claims charge and see what he does. Whatever it is, it'll tell us something. If you want, tell him you've named me your proxy in all matters relating to the federal case, and his acquisition offer. I'll do the work. Insulate yourself and force him to deal with me. I'll flush him out."

"Okay," she said, then got out of the lounge chair and shook out her hair, combing her fingers through the thick mass. She took a few steps over to the edge of the pool and dove in. I walked over there and watched her swim through the pool lights to the bottom, skim along the floor, then push off for the surface. When she burst through, she held her nose and dipped her head into the water, slicking back her hair. In the up lit glow, her face was both familiar and strange, a version of someone you thought you knew.

"Coming in?" she asked.

"Can't swim."

"You're lying."

"No, just can't swim tonight. Have to go home and get some rest."

She performed a graceful breaststroke over to the side of the pool, and with little hesitation, hoisted herself out of the water, which splashed around her, darkening the slate tile. I found a towel in a cabinet a few feet away and handed it to her. She held it, but didn't dry off. Her dress was now a second skin, revealing a surprisingly girlish shape. I took the towel out of her hand and wrapped it over her shoulders, pressing her into a protective hug.

"You've lost a lot of weight," I said.

"The grief diet," she said. "Very effective. I should write a book. Step one, get your husband murdered."

"You meant be married to a murdered husband."

"I did," she said, laying her head against my chest. "I just keep feeling responsible."

"Survivor's guilt. They can treat you for that."

"I don't want to be treated. I just want him back."

I walked her toward the house, rubbing her skin through the towel. When we were inside, she pulled away and tossed the towel off her shoulders. Facing away from me, she slithered out of the dress, letting if fall into a puddle on the floor. I watched her naked body move through the living room toward the hall that led to the bedrooms.

As soon as she was out of sight, I left.

CHAPTER TWENTY

For some reason, I couldn't face the condo after leaving Megan's place. I'm usually fine with solitude, but sometimes the silence becomes a clamor of its own kind, and I needed ambient light and noise to distract me from my runaway inner dialogue.

So I drove the Harley around for a while, until I found myself near Skinny McDowell's, and went in to have a drink, like a normal single person. It was later than usual for me, and my regular crowd was long gone. So I picked a spot at the bar away from the ubiquitous big-screen TVs and ordered a beer.

By my second beer, the area surrounding the bar began to fill up, with no more available seating. The clientele was mostly young men, with baseball caps, unneeded vests and clumps of keys hanging by straps from their belts. Many of the women wore tank tops and jeans a size too small. They were all clearly enjoying themselves, and I found the burble of jovial conversation soothing.

I rarely went past a couple of drinks, not liking the physical effects of excess. Not so my brother, who had an impressive capacity, both for quantity and heights of joyfulness. My role, when we were through high school and college, was to keep an eye on him and get him safely home. No matter what trouble he managed to inspire with his reckless abandon.

I had nearly finished my second, and final, beer when the crowd behind me grew to where I was getting jostled. The offenders apologized, but it was clearly time for me to give up the seat and get out of there. I put enough money on the bar to cover the beers and tip, and pushed away from the bar, nudging into the two guys immediately behind me. When I stood up, they blocked my way. They were taller than I am, and seemed to be enjoying my struggle to get past.

I moved to the left, and they moved the same way, grinning. And swaying a little, as you do when there's been a few beers too many. I moved to the right, and they repeated their response. One of them flipped my lapel, I think a socioeconomic statement, since I was in a sport coat and button-down collar shirt, and he wasn't. I didn't react, so he flipped it again, this time swiping my chin. He called me something ungracious, but I couldn't exactly hear it over the music.

I put my left hand on the guy's shoulder and shouted, "My name's Waters. What's yours?"

He said something I couldn't hear, but I said, "Nice to meet you," and stuck out my hand. When he took it, I squeezed. The power of a grip is mostly in the forearm, but if you concentrate, you can direct some extra energy down from the rest of the arm and shoulder. I felt around for his knuckles, putting them somewhat out of alignment, then bore down. He tried to pull away, but I held on until his knees buckled and his face showed panicked alarm.

When I let go, I used my left hand, still on his shoulder, to gently shove him out of my way. As I moved past I told him he could have my seat.

No one seemed to think it was worth following me out of the bar, so I left the parking lot unimpeded and took in the pleasures of the warm summer air, made into wind by the Harley's acceleration, washing across my face.

Megan Rajput never got a chance to tell Sarnac about the Federal False Claims charge against ExciteAble. When I got to work, he was in our lobby with three other people, two men and one woman, in dark suits carrying plain leather briefcases. Carmine Fusco was standing next to the receptionist who pretended to work at her computer.

Sarnac was in full umbrage mode.

"She refused to see us without you in the room," he said.

I nodded to Carmine and he had the receptionist call up to Megan. She directed us to the main conference room. Carmine led the way, I took up the rear. The parade drew a few furtive looks, and people stepped aside as we moved down the halls in single file.

Megan, dressed in a man's shirt and jeans, obviously hadn't expected formal company. She sat at the head of the conference table with a bottle of water and pad of paper. There were no greetings or small talk. Sarnac and crew sat on one side of the table, I took the other. Carmine bowed out.

"I am extremely upset, Megan," said Sarnac.

"You mean Mrs. Rajput."

She took a sip of her water, hands steady.

Sarnac kept his eyes on Megan and held his hand out to the lawyer sitting next to him. The lawyer gave him an envelope. Sarnac removed a letter and smoothed the creases on the table.

"If even half of what the contents of this letter alleges is true, ExciteAble Technologies is facing an existential threat," he said. "As chairman of the board of directors, and a 5 percent shareholder, I have specific and personal liability for the so-called fraudulent actions taken by this company."

"Bullshit, Nelson," she said, cutting him off. "You're only liable if you had knowledge of, or participated in, the alleged fraud. We'll cover your legal costs to prove you had nothing to do with it. Though one lawyer and maybe a paralegal should be enough."

Sarnac looked across the table at me.

"Why is he here?" he asked.

"That's not your concern," she said.

"The bloody hell it isn't. Was he part of the scam?"

I looked at the lawyer sitting beside him, and said, "First, we'll need a copy of that letter. Second, Mrs. Rajput, as majority shareholder, will be suspending Mr. Sarnac's position as board chair effective immediately."

Sarnac slapped the table with both hands.

"On what grounds?"

"Your offer to acquire ExciteAble is in direct conflict with your fiduciary role as a director," I said. "We were going to allow you to recuse yourself from the negotiations, but since you're here threatening legal action, a seat on our board is untenable. We have nothing further to discuss with you today. Communications going forward will be handled through our corporate counsel, and I presume you," I said, looking at his lawyer, "who appear to be representing Mr. Sarnac. We'll just need your contact information."

He slid his card across the table. "And what is your position here?" he asked.

"Senior Vice President for Administration," said Megan. "Second only to me. It's a very recent promotion. We'll get you his new cards as soon as they're printed up."

"A shyster promotes a con artist," said Sarnac. "Figures."

"Fuck you very much, Nelson," said Megan. She stood up and went to the door, where Carmine was waiting. When he came into the room, she asked him to escort our visitors out of the building.

It looked like Sarnac wasn't finished talking, but Megan bent down and put her index finger on his lips. "Don't say anything now, Nelson. You'll only regret it later."

Carmine gestured with both hands for them to rise, and then herded them out of the room. I heard him say, "Ladies first. Head down the hall and turn left. Be right behind you."

When they were out of earshot, I asked Megan if we had corporate counsel.

"One of Paresh's cousins. Way over his head. Your first act as SVP is finding us a new one."

"You didn't have to promote me," I said. "I'd help you anyway."

"I know. It just kinda popped into my head. You deserve it, but it's also important for you to have the authority to deal with Sarnac and give orders to everyone in the organization. I trust you to know when to ask me and when to just go ahead and do shit. You can add crisis management to your résumé when we go down the tubes."

Looking far less formidable than she did a few minutes before, I wanted her to know that she'd handled the situation perfectly.

"Thanks, Waters. What about Sarnac, what can he do?"

"Not sure, but he might cause more trouble as a share-holder than a director. He's a lot richer than I thought."

I told her about my little drive around with the private detective. "Paresh made him chairman mostly to get access to his money," she said. "There was a time when the only thing keeping us afloat was Nelson Sarnac. But I never liked him. Always smelled of cigars and bad aftershave, two things at the top of my hate list."

She took a deep breath and headed toward the door. I opened it for her.

"Before I go home tonight, I'm stopping at the church, lighting a few candles, and praying to Saint Jude. You probably don't know what that means."

I admitted I didn't.

"He's the saint of lost causes. I want him to take a look at our case. Is that ridiculous or what?"

I told her it wasn't.

"A successful CEO avails herself of any ally she can. Especially in times of duress," I said.

She drew her hand down the side of my face.

"That's exactly what they taught us in Catholic school. How did you know?"

———— • ————

JADEEN KNOX said she'd help with the False Claims case if she hadn't nearly died of boredom studying corporate law. She said her firm had a business practice but thought we wouldn't gel. Too white shoe and country club for an oddball like me. Her favorite professor, on the other hand, the one that got her through the agony of those courses and became her closest mentor, would fit the bill nicely.

"He's an old hippie, teaches and keeps a small practice to stay current."

She gave me his private e-mail address and said to wait a day for her to clear a path. I did as she asked, then sent him a message that briefly described our situation. I got this back:

"If Jadeen says you're cool, I'm cool. Here's the way-point. I'm good tomorrow from noon on. Wear boat shoes."

The GPS on my phone pegged the address as a spot in the middle of Sheffield Harbor, a body of water off Rowayton, the verdant, suburban throwback south of Norwalk, Connecticut. I took the Harley over there and ferreted out the harbormaster, who had Professor Santo's mooring in his log. He referred me to a boat taxi that could get me out there, endorsing her nautical skills and reasonable pricing. He suggested I bring along a few bags of ice, Italian sausage and cheese, a carton of Marlboros, and six-pack of hard lemonade, all items he knew the professor frequently requested of his friend who provisioned the harbor boats.

"He'll love you for it," he said. "Guaranteed."

So it took me about an hour to travel around the mainland, acquire and stuff all the goods into my backpack, which I brought with me on the short taxi ride to Santo's sailboat, a fifty-three-foot schooner moored at the outer edge of the bay.

I was a little surprised to see a tiny Japanese man catch our line as we crept up to the stern of his boat. I was expecting something more Spanish. I heaved my backpack into the cockpit, handed the taxi operator her fee plus 20 percent, and clamored up the swim ladder. I was greeted by a Portuguese water dog who seemed inordinately glad to have company. Santo took my hand into both of his and bowed.

"Please forgive the dog," he said, "she tires of me. I should let her go off with the next stranger she fawns over and see how she likes it. Thanks for all the stuff. You like tea? I just found this Sumatra Black some graduate student at Cal Tech genetically engineered to taste like licorice and produce twice the caffeine."

"Sure."

The boat was the equivalent of an old main street bank. Sturdy as a rock, fine materials and craftsmanship, deeply worn but well maintained. Serenely spare and organized, unlike its owner, whose silk running shorts hung off him like a loin cloth, and whose unkempt grey hair could have been hiding a family of small birds.

I followed him below. The cabin upheld the fastidiousness shown topside. Though sunlight filled the space, candles warmed the colors, deepening the dark amber tones of teak woodwork. A pot was heating on the galley stove. He motioned me to sit in the salon and disappeared forward for a few minutes, then came back with his hair wet and combed into place, wearing a dark blue sweat suit and yellow Crocs on his feet.

"How's' Jadeen?" he asked, as he prepared the tea.

"I don't know her well enough to know," I said.

He looked over his shoulder at me.

"One of my favorite people," he said. "The only student to throw a houseplant at me when I told her she was in danger of flunking my course."

"What did you do?"

"I threw it back at her. Didn't miss." He handed me the tea in an antique Wedgewood coffee cup. "Take the bag out when I tell you to. Wait too long and you'll be up for three days."

I smelled a thick aroma billowing from the ornate cup.

"Our company is in a pretty serious jam. We need fresh corporate counsel," I said.

"Jadeen told me that already," he said, dropping into the opposite settee and pulling his legs into a lotus position. "Tell me something she doesn't know."

"The CEO wants to sleep with me. I think it's only a primal urge to be intimate with the person she thinks has the best shot at saving her company, though she's fatalistic about that."

"Saving the company or having sex with you?"

"Both."

"Take out the tea bag and start at the beginning, if you don't mind."

Having grown in length and dimension, the story took a while to recount. I assumed he was listening carefully, since he barely moved or took notes, just stared into the tea cup, which he held near his face with both hands. When I was finished, he started asking questions, beginning with the night Paresh was murdered. As he asked more questions, it was evident he'd absorbed every word of my story. I tried to answer thoroughly, assuming he wanted every detail.

Three hours and two more cups of tea later, he said, "Okay. I'll take the case." And gave a little bow. I bowed back.

"Thank you," I said. "Is that all for now?"

"Unless you have questions for me."

"Do you own a suit?"

"Brooks Brothers."

"What's your real name?"

"Sato. The Latino kids I grew up with in California found it easier to say Santo, so I figured, what the hell, and stuck with it."

"I'd like you to meet with Megan," I said. "It's not an audition. I've made my decision, I just want you to know her as a person. It's her life we're trying to save."

"And your life?"

"Incidental. I'll send you some dates and times. While you're there, we can plan on next steps. Interviews, document review, whatever. Bring the dog."

I stood up and would have shaken his hand, but he stepped in and gave me a full wraparound hug. I didn't know what to do, so I just stood there. When he didn't let go, I hugged him back. His muscles were thick, and surprisingly firm for a man his age.

"No lives are incidental, son," he said, finally releasing me. "You'll miss it when it's gone."

Before I went back to ExciteAble, I stopped by Los Umbros to get a status report. Their offices were in an ancient stone building that had started life as a foundry sometime in the nineteenth century, now fully restored and home to a dozen small businesses. Billy's wife greeted me like I was a cousin who'd just moved back to town after ten years in Alaska. She said Billy was out on a job, but Glen was around, and fully up to speed on the case.

He joined me in the conference room carrying a stack of files and a laptop. Wearing an undersized dark blue T-shirt and black jeans, he looked more like a bouncer, or car mechanic, than a private investigator. Maybe he was all those things.

He carefully laid the files out on the table and spent a moment putting them in the proper sequence. He let me know he was more of the inside computer search guy, and Billy more the surveillance, follow people around town, slug assholes in the face guy, so it was just as well that I caught him in the office.

Once he was all organized, he sat down, flipped open the computer and said, "Miss Alexander led a very active life. In addition to an impressive list of employers, qualitatively and quantitatively, she put a lot of time into physical fitness involving multiple health clubs, gyms, team sports, and social organizations, some of which included adventure tours abroad and international tennis and golf matches. Her activities were not confined to athletics, however. She also participated in chess tournaments, adult spelling bees and math competitions, and game show auditions, nearly landing a spot on *Jeopardy!*"

This came as no surprise to me. Glen continued.

"Consistent with her employment history, most of these engagements featured nonpayment of dues, fees, and cost sharing, fraudulent membership applications, and in a few instances, outright cheating, as when she took a bus for half a bike race in Bermuda. I really wish I'd met this girl. As long as I was armed."

"What about her associations," I said.

"That's the fun part for me," he said, patting his laptop like you would the head of a young child. "It takes a lot of time, but I keep a running tally of names that appear along with hers and copy them into the data base. Copy and paste when I can, brute force data entry when I can't. That's bad for me. I type with two fingers, maximum. Harder still, I tag each of the names by number of appearances, and length of association. That's what really takes the most time. Computers are fast when you got the data, nobody talks about the poor schmucks who put the data there in the first place."

He looked down at the computer screen.

"I'm up to around a thousand names so far, believe it or not," he said. He looked up. "Though if you think about it, Yolanda spent her life jumping from one situation to another. You can rack up a lot of associations that way, without knowing them all that long. I'd call it sad if Yolanda actually gave a shit about these people and didn't want them to disappear from her life as quickly as possible."

He worked at the computer for a while, staring intently and tapping away, in a manner that caused others, I'd observed, to boil with frustration. I often wondered what was so hard about sitting and waiting. I enjoyed sitting and waiting, feeling the slowing of time until it collapsed into stasis, a

pause in the march of the general order. A place where you
could hear the air, see the hum of light passing through the
physical world. Feel the tap-tap-tap of computer keys.

"So, Waters," he said, finally. I felt time restart. "I've
been resisting the analysis until I had a critical mass of
data. Partly because, why jump ahead when things are only
going to change? Partly because it's fun to wait. Delayed
gratification."

He stared some more at the computer.

"I think it's pretty interesting," he said, "but I'll let you
be the judge. I'm printing it out. Be right back."

When he left, I occupied myself looking at the kids'
drawings pinned to the wall. I knew people saw brilliance
in their children's random scribbling, which was understandable. But usually, it wasn't genius on display, but rather the
manifestation of helpless, uncontrollable love.

Glen came back in the room and put a piece of paper
on the table in front of me. He sat down with his own copy.

"This is a very simple program, probably one of the ear-
liest analytics applications ever written. What you see are
correlations. There're ranked here by order of frequency
and duration. None of them mean anything to me, but they
might to you."

He was right about the simplicity of the report. A single
column of about fifty names running down the left margin.
The next column to the right reporting the degree of cor-
relation between Yolanda and another person, and a third
column noting how long the association had existed.

I scanned my eyes down the page, seeing Belinda at the
top. My name was near the bottom, as were Paresh's and
Megan Rajput's, and Jack Warner's. I looked for more familiar names until I was back to the one directly below Belinda's.

Nelson Sarnac.

Chapter Twenty-One

I spent the next few nights driving past Reece & Reece headquarters in Branford. On the third night, I caught the cleaning service as they were pulling into the driveway. Only one man got out of the van, hauling a vacuum cleaner. I stopped the Harley and watched him enter the building. Lights flicked on as he moved around. It was all I needed to see, so I drove off.

The next night, I went back to Reece & Reece, this time a half hour before the cleaning guy would show up, if he kept to the same schedule. I parked in the lot behind the building. He was punctual, and I was ready to follow him as he struggled through the door with the vacuum cleaner.

"What the hell?" he said, when I grabbed him by the collar and dragged him to the double-door entrance to Reece & Reece. I told him to open it, which he did promptly.

"I will not hurt you, I promise," I said. "I just need to look around for a bit. But I have to keep you secure while I do that. Okay?"

"Not really, man. I'm supposed to be cleaning this place."

"I know. I'll be as fast as I can. I'm really sorry."

I took him and his vacuum to the conference room where I'd chatted with Joel Reece and left him sitting on the floor tied with worn clothesline to a leg of the conference room table. I put five hundred dollars in his shirt pocket.

"I know it's meager compensation for the shock and trouble, but it makes me feel better to do something," I said.

"In that case, what else you got in your wallet?"

I checked.

"About another hundred bucks."

"Well, put that in, too, and I'll forget what you look like."

"Deal," I said, and added the other bills.

I left him and started to explore the offices. There were no name plates on the walls, but it was easy to identify the owners of individual offices through a quick check of papers scattered around the desks, tables, and credenzas. It wasn't long before I came to a big office with mahogany furniture, expensive executive games, and Oriental rugs on the floor. A large window overlooked the harbor. A framed caricature of Joel Reece swinging a golf club, signed by Tiger Woods, was on the wall behind the desk. Photographs of Reece and his family were on the desk, facing out like advertisements for his successful domestic life. I went through the only cabinet in the room and found a file marked "Olivia."

I pulled a soft bag out of my back pocket and stuck in the folder. Then moved on.

An office two doors down had an in-basket full of mail addressed to Olivia Lefèvre. I searched the file tabs for any familiar names, to no avail. Then I came on a file titled "Personal Stuff." I almost took it, but it felt like a violation, so I left it and went back to the conference room and my captured cleaning guy. He didn't look too worse for the wear. I sat on the floor next to him.

"Got what you wanted?" he asked.

"I don't know yet. I moved as fast as I could."

"That's good. I got two more buildings to do tonight."

I untied him and helped him to his feet. He rubbed his wrists and told me I had a lot to learn about tying people up.

"Coulda slipped out of them knots the second you was gone."

"I didn't want to cause too much discomfort," I said.

We shook hands, wished each other luck, and I was out of there. I strapped the bag with Olivia's file to a rack above the Harley's rear wheel and took off.

I stayed well within the speed limits as I worked my way up through New Haven and out to my condominium. My first breaking and entering, with a dose of kidnapping, had gone well. I told myself not to make a habit of it, and my counter-self told me to shut up and keep driving.

When I got to the condo, I opened Joel Reece's file marked "Olivia." It began with her application to the firm, a number of years before, along with a cover letter where she eloquently outlined her unique skills and qualifications. None of them were related to executive recruiting. Rather, typing skills, knowledge of office software, outgoing personality, and good work ethic.

She was applying to be Joel Reece's administrative assistant.

Attached were three references. All were character testimonials, one from an attorney in New York, apparently a friend of Reece's, whose commentary was short, but ended with a request for Reece to give her a call.

About six months later, he wrote Olivia a note thanking her for doing a great job, exceeding his expectations. She memoed back her thanks for the appreciation.

A year after that, she applied to become a full-time recruiter, citing her deepening involvement in the process and frequent service as his proxy, freeing him to spend more time with key candidates. He told her she beat him to it and proposed a draw against commissions. She came back and asked for all commission at a higher percentage, so confident was she in her ability to pay her way.

Subsequent memos told of a steady rise in her responsibilities, status, commission rates, and all the other signposts of a successful climb. And the tone changed, still warm, but with the familiarity of colleagues, nearly peers. Plenty of humor. His stiff, hers witty and facile.

I felt a little lift of my heart reading her prose, which sounded so much like her voice to my inner ear.

Interspersed were e-mails that discussed various openings, and her strategies for filling them. Eventually, I arrived at her most recent correspondence.

"As we discussed, I have some personal things to deal with that might take me out of the office for several weeks. I'm only asking for a sabbatical, without pay, not including whatever commissions are already coming to me. I can't leave a forwarding address and won't be using e-mail, but I'll have a cell phone with me. You have the number, but please DO NOT SHARE WITH ANYONE.

"I love being part of your team, and hope I've held up my side of the bargain. Your faith in me is everything, and I will never do anything to lose that."

Also included was his response.

"You know how I feel. Take all the time you want. The light is always on. (And your office always waiting.)"

While I was spending my nights casing Reece & Reece, my days were filled with meetings among Megan, Brice, and Santo, whom I started calling Santosan, to his barely hidden delight. He'd camped out in our management war room where we had him set up with a computer and big chart paper mounted to an easel.

The first day he showed up in his Brooks Brothers suit, but subsequently in classic business casual, which he told me was a show of respect for our engineering culture. He hit it off with Megan and Brice immediately, to whom he expressed a seductive blend of brilliance and humility, subtly pitched to their personalities.

The day after I boosted the paperwork from Reece & Reece, we gathered with Santosan for a planning meeting.

"First," he said, "let me commend you all on the quality of your processes and procedures, and impeccable record keeping. You don't know how rare it is, even among supposedly top-flight companies."

Megan thanked him.

"But let's start with corporate governance. You've adhered well to your charter and bylaws, which are appropriate to this type of privately held operation. As I've already noted, as the majority stockholder, Megan was within her prerogatives to suspend Mr. Sarnac from the board. In fact, suspension as opposed to full removal was an intelligent approach."

She thanked him again. He gave a little bow.

"With this firm foundation, you are well positioned to mount a vigorous defense against the Federal False Claims action, having demonstrated the characteristics of a well-managed, responsible company." He smiled at Megan. "And that, I'm afraid, is the end of the good news."

She stiffened.

"As Colin has nicely laid out, the fraud was hidden inside normal billing and accounting activities, by employees of the company, led by Miss Alexander. At the end of every month, she cleared everything with Paresh, who signed off without comment. Clean and simple, and seemingly intentional, willful, and flagrantly illegal."

Stillness settled on the room. We'd heard this before, but with Santosan uttering the words, the situation took on a tangibility, and finality, we hadn't felt before.

"Let's get back to the good news," said Megan. "What do you say?"

Santosan's face wrinkled with amusement.

"The best news is you have me to plead your case. I'm very good at that. We also have a perpetrator with a long history of criminality and fraud, identified thanks to Dr. Waters's investigative efforts. Proving means and opportunity is a simple task. What we don't have is motive. Unless we agree with the prosecutors that she was working for Paresh, whose means and opportunity are also clear, and sadly, so is motive—to financially benefit his company."

"Paresh wouldn't do that," said Megan. "Not in a million, trillion years."

"That is stipulated within these walls," said Santosan. "And though I never had the pleasure of knowing Mr. Rajput, I've seen nothing about his company that suggests illicit behavior. I've defended corporate executives whose impulses were nearly always to do the wrong thing. Paresh shows the opposite."

I thought Megan might begin to tear up, but Brice stole our attention.

"And he didn't have to," he said. "Paresh had absolutely no reason to jeopardize everything just to squeeze a few hundred thousand dollars out of the government."

Santosan stood up and went over to where the easel stood with a clean sheet of chart paper.

"If I was a prosecutor speaking to a jury," said Santosan, "I would say, 'We will prove beyond a reasonable doubt that Paresh Rajput, with his accomplice, Yolanda Alexander, defrauded the government and used the ill-gotten gains to pay off the defendant, Dr. Waters, who was extorting him, who subsequently murdered Mr. Rajput, and Ms. Alexander, in order to cover up the scheme and evade justice.'"

My brother once tried to explain to me why a ten-year-old kid at the special school I was going to at the time could beat any adult at chess, even professional competitors, but didn't know how to speak, get dressed, eat with utensils, or ride a bike. He said, pretend chess was the color blue. The kid could see blue better than anyone else. However, except for blue, the kid was colorblind. No greens, reds or yellows. That's just the way he was born.

I asked my brother what colors I could see. He said I was pretty good with greens, reds, and yellows, but for me, there was a lot of blue out there that I just couldn't see. Not yet, anyway.

At that moment, in the company war room, I felt like the whole world was painted in multiple shades of blue.

"That's ridiculous," said Megan. "This is a forty-million-dollar company. There are dozens of ways Paresh could have legitimately funded payments to Waters. Christ, he could've written a personal check, then reimbursed himself with a bonus. He handled all our finances. I'd never know. It's just nuts."

Santosan sat back down at the table and said, "As the psychologist on the team, perhaps Dr. Waters can help us understand what's nuts, and what isn't."

Before my brother could start telling me stories as we ran around the woods behind our house, he had to explain the difference between a story that was true, and one that wasn't. This was jarring to me at the time, since I'd assumed everything he said was true. I finally grasped the concept when he told me a story that was purely factual and asked me how it made me feel. I said it made me feel good. Then he told it again, this time filled with embellishments and imaginative twists and turns and asked how that felt. I said, really, really great.

"A story doesn't have to be true," I said. "It just has to appear to be true. It's all about the narrative, the facts are incidental."

"Exactly what I tell my students who want to be trial lawyers," said Santosan. "Nothing beats a great story."

CHAPTER TWENTY-TWO

The next day, Megan received an olive branch. Literally.
Nelson Sarnac had someone place an actual olive branch on
a velvet pillow inside a finely crafted mahogany box. With
the branch was a note that said, "We got off on the wrong
foot the other day. My fault. Please let's try again."

She and I sat in her office staring at the box.

"What do you think?" she asked.

"I think you say sure, why not."

"I don't trust him," she said,

"You don't have to trust him. You just have to listen."

She picked up the box and walked it over to a file cabinet
with long horizontal drawers. She pulled open the bottom
drawer, tossed in the box, and shut the drawer with her foot.

"Okay. Set it up."

That night at the condo, I shut off the AC and sat out on
the little balcony that overlooked a meager patch of gnarly
overgrowth and listened for any lifeforms strident enough to
overcome the wash of human noise rising up from the city.
I tried to settle my mind, but it was too clamorous, despite
the soothing world around me. A thought was growing up
from deep inside me, but it had yet to declare itself. A voice
was speaking to me, but I couldn't hear what it was saying.

It was keeping me awake, but there was nothing I could do about it, so I went to bed to get the tossing and turning underway.

———— • ————

NELSON SARNAC only brought one lawyer with him this time, the young lady. On our side of the table was Megan, Santosan, and myself. Sarnac and Santosan had met each other a few times in the past, and each professed admiration for the other's achievements. The ExciteAble contingent was in professional garb, conservative suits and ties, with Megan in a high-collared blouse that recalled the 1980s.

Sarnac repeated the words in the note, emphasizing his culpability in the matter. Megan thanked him for that, and said she bore responsibility for not informing him of the False Claims charge sooner, for which she apologized. Sarnac also said he accepted his suspension from the board as necessary while a possible acquisition was on the table. Which he hoped was still the case.

Megan nodded.

"We are open to discussing it," she said.

Sarnac looked relieved. He glanced at his lawyer and she nodded, as if giving him permission to proceed.

"I went home that night after the meeting and did some soul searching," he said. "Better than that, I did some phone calling. Close to fifty years of managing government contracts has to be good for something. I have a lot of friends down in DC, working and retired. I presented the situation, no names of course, just as a theoretical."

"Not with the DOD officials involved in our case, presumably," said Santosan.

"No. Just people who know the process."

Santosan nodded. Sarnac took a deep breath, gathering his words.

"The situation isn't as dire as it appears," he said, "depending on what sort of agreement we can come to. If we can prove that the fraudulent activity had never occurred before, that it was confined to a narrow list of contracts, and engaged in by a limited number of individuals, without the knowledge of the management team, we have a shot."

"One of those individuals was the company's CEO," said Santosan. "Not an insignificant member of senior management."

Sarnac clasped his hands and bowed his head, as if ready to launch into prayer.

"This is the painful part, Megan, and I hope you'll forgive me, but it's pivotal to addressing the situation."

"I think I know where you're going," she said. "The people allegedly involved in the fraud are both dead. We prove it begins and ends with them, we can return to the air force's good graces."

"In a nutshell, yes. Though there's a bit more to it," said Sarnac.

Santosan asked if he could hypothesize what that bit would be. Sarnac nodded.

"We agree that the fraud took place and warrant that it was unprecedented and never to be repeated. We will settle on the substance of the charges and pay a civil fine. We will submit to more frequent audits for a period of time, at our expense. And, if experience in these matters is any guide, the air force will insist on a restructuring at the management level."

Sarnac looked sad to concur.

"The prosecutors will want a few sacrificial lambs, to put it bluntly," he said. "This ultimately comes down to politics. And in politics, the optics are everything."

Megan's freckles deepened in color, but her posture was unchanged. We waited for her to respond.

"Which lambs, I suppose, would have to be determined," she said.

"Of course," said Sarnac. "But I have a way to work that out."

Again, Santosan asked if he could speculate on Sarnac's proposal. Sarnac agreed with a wave of his hand.

"You will make the purchase of ExciteAble a part of the settlement with the government. By doing so, you assume all debts and obligations, including any impending civil fines, and assume responsibility for ongoing management. This assures the government that ExciteAble is made financially secure, guaranteeing no further attempt to defraud, and with new oversight, inoculated against the political need for bloodletting."

"That is correct," said Sarnac, slapping both hands on the table, with a grin, the first sign that the Sarnac we all knew was still lurking in there. The female lawyer looked at Santosan warmly.

"And naturally," Santosan added, "the price you previously offered for ExciteAble will have to be adjusted downward in order to offset these new, rather significant, expenses."

"Regrettably, yes," he said. "But I think you'll still be happy, Megan. I plan to retain you as CEO and leave all other management decisions in your hands." He paused and looked over at me. "Yield a decent annual return, grow the bottom line, which you're clearly capable of doing, and all is well. Or ride off into the sunset, your choice."

Megan sunk a little in her seat, her expression uncharacteristically blank, but she didn't flinch or avert her eyes as he spoke. Santosan was implacable as a hunk of granite.

"I never pictured you riding in on a white horse, Nelson," said Megan. "But now it's getting easier."

"I actually own a white horse, Megan. If you want, next time I'll bring him along."

She slid her gaze over to Santosan, who nodded.

"This is a lot to digest," she said to Sarnac. "I truly appreciate your generous offer. I just need to huddle with my team before discussing next steps."

Enough magnanimity flowed from Sarnac to nearly flood the room.

"Take all the time you want," he said. "Understanding that the government works on their schedule, not ours. I'm ready to complete formalities whenever you are."

He stood up and everyone shook hands across the table, difficult for Sarnac, since he had very short arms. The young female lawyer, who hadn't said a word, brushed her fingertips across my palm when she let go. Otherwise, the exchange was pro forma, and within a few minutes we had the conference room back to ourselves.

Megan flopped down in her chair and said, "Fuck a duck and the horse he rode in on."

Santosan stood there silently.

"Out with it, you two. What do you think?"

Santosan tried to defer to me, but I shook my head.

"On the face of it," he said, "an excellent deal. Based on what I know, his assumptions about the federal case are well founded. The government loves to toss smaller companies into the arms of bigger companies, who have deeper pockets for sure, and better management skills, probably not. But it's all so clean and simple, and politically expedient, that these deals almost always sail through without a hitch."

Santosan had the smell of a man waiting through a tedious lunch with his wife and her friends so he could get to the golf course by tee time.

"You think we should go for it," I said.

He reached across the table and rested his hand on my forearm.

"I do, Dr. Waters. For Megan's sake. You may never find a happier job, but you'll land on your feet, and have many years to prove your worth."

This alarmed Megan.

"Sarnac said I could make all executive decisions," she said. "That includes who I want in management."

He let go of my arm, and with his elbows on the table, pointed two index fingers in her direction.

"I hate to break it to you, Mrs. Rajput," he said, "but the last son of a bitch Sarnac wants to deal with, if he can help it, is Dr. Waters. Am I right?" he asked me.

"You are," I said to Megan. "And like he said, I'll be fine."

She combed her hair back with her fingers and looked down at the table.

"I know. You'll be fine. Not sure about me."

I went home late that night, unsure if I should leave Megan alone at the office, but she didn't call me in, and when I saw her Mercedes missing from the lot, I felt free to go.

I waited until eating and drinking my two or three nightly beers to go online and check in on ChatJazz. Plato had left a post two days before:

"Tired of me? Don't want to play anymore? I'm tired of you too. I think you need to go away. You're no fun at all."

I usually waited a few days to craft my response, but it didn't seem worth it at that point. I was exhausted from the day, and worried about Olivia, and maybe a little frustrated trying to play the behavior of that cruel, selfish bastard, so I ignored years of psychological training and wrote, "You're backing off because I'm getting closer, and you know it. You don't have the balls to up the game. So slither back into your hole, you piece of shit. I'll follow you down there and wring your scrawny neck."

An hour after hitting send, an angry bee flew past my face and went thup into the living room wall. Two more bees followed in quick succession. I shoved backward off my chair and onto the floor. My flat-screen monitor exploded, spraying me and the room with tiny electronic shards. Something knocked into my thigh, half spinning me around. I wriggled over to the seating area as other items in the room burst into molecules, killing lamps and throwing the room into near darkness. I angled a love seat so it stood between me and the window, and felt it bump violently as successive rounds ripped into the soft upholstery.

I lay as flat as I could on the floor and listened to the pattern of the bullet spray, trying to calculate if it was closing in on me, or moving away. A fire alarm went off somewhere in the building. I prayed no one on my hall thought they should come see what all the banging was about.

I took the little automatic out of my rear waistband. Not a sniper's rifle, but far better than nothing. I peered around the side of the love seat and saw a flash from the building across the parking lot. Propped up on my elbows, I emptied the clip in the direction of the flash, then crawled deeper into the room, moving away from the love seat and putting the full length of the sofa between me and the window. I propped my back against the end of the sofa and waited. A faint hope was quenched when a dozen more rounds ripped the love seat into a cloud of shredded fabric and stuffing. So I stayed put at the end of the sofa, which seemed to offer an adequate defense, and called Detective Shapiro.

"Gunfire," I said, when he answered. "I could use a little help."

At that moment the window blew out, crashing giant slabs of glass onto the hardwood floor. Which Shapiro obviously heard.

"On the way," he said.

I just lay there, listening to the occasional slap of a high-velocity bullet hit something in the condo. Then the bullets stopped as a bunch of guys in bulky blue jump suits crept into the condo, yelling for me to stay in place. Which I was glad to do. It was then that the burning sensation in my right thigh got a lot worse and I tasted something metallic running across my lips.

For some reason, I wondered if I'd turned off the coffee maker, thinking I'd be away from the condo for a while, before sliding effortlessly into unconsciousness.

Chapter Twenty-Three

The trouble with waking up in a hospital is you never actually wake up. At least not right away. You just slowly emerge from this woolly fog, if you're lucky. A dry throat, screaming headache, and serious need to piss, if you're not.

I woke to all the above.

A woman in a surgical mask and hairnet squinted at me through thick, plastic-framed glasses. I tried to say boo but couldn't muster the strength. She grabbed my wrist and looked over at a bank of monitors. I told her I had to take a piss. She shook her head as if she didn't understand me, which figured, since I couldn't understand myself.

I pointed at my groin.

She said, "Just let it go. You're catheterized."

Oh, no, I thought, trying to lean up so I could see what they'd done to me. She gently pushed me back onto the bed.

"Stay still," she said. "We have to check your vitals. The doctor is on her way."

Something was sticking to my forehead. I reached up and felt gauze. When I lifted my arms, tentacles yanked at them, pulling on the skin. The woman told me again not to move around so much.

"Mind those IVs," she said. "They come out of there and we'll have a bloody mess."

I realized she had a British accent. How did I get to England, I wondered. Airlift? If so, why?

I heard myself ask for water. She gave me a straw to suck on. The lukewarm water was like an exotic, life-restoring elixir. I grabbed the cup and made her let me draw another few mouthfuls.

"Throat," I croaked, letting go of the cup.

"You had an intubation tube," she said. "Better than suffocating under anesthesia."

"Agreed," I said.

"You are quite strong," she said. "If you don't cooperate, I shall have to order up some burly chaps."

I said I was sorry. No chaps of any kind necessary. I just wanted to know where I was.

"Yale New Haven Hospital," she said. "In the Intensive Care Unit."

"So not Nottingham or Chichester?"

"I'm from Hampstead in North London, if you must know," she said.

"I was just about to say that."

The doctor was a minute Latina who looked about fourteen. I noticed she had to roll up the sleeves of her white coat to free her hands. Her bedside manner was practiced, but at least she gave it a go. She asked me if I knew what had happened to me. I said not really.

"You sustained a bullet wound to your thigh, in and out. All muscle, no big veins or arteries. And a piece of glass was embedded in your scalp, just inside the hairline. It was removed surgically."

I wondered what other way it could have been removed. Telekinesis?

"We have to check the wounds and change the bandages. There will be some pain. Do you want additional painkillers?"

I said no way, and in a few minutes regretted that decision. But I kept it to myself. My brother always told me, never let them see you suffer, never let them see you cry. I wasn't going to start at that late date.

Anyway, one of the tubes hooked to my arm was probably dumping plenty of narcotic directly into my bloodstream, which partly explained why my mood was more appropriate to a New Year's Eve celebration than a stay in the ICU.

"How soon can I walk out of here?" I asked.

"Not too long," said the doctor. "It was a small-caliber round, with a heavy charge. So it made a nice, small, straight hole through the soft tissue. Likely an assault rifle. Military grade. No evidence of infection. You picked a lucky way to be shot."

"All things considered," I said.

"We're moving you to a room in a few minutes," said the nurse. "Under police escort you'll be pleased to know."

"Really?"

"The young man is right outside the ICU," she said, "frightening the other patients, to say nothing of staff."

On the way to the room, I asked the cop if he could let Shapiro know I was awake, punchy, but awake. And eager to have a talk. He radioed the dispatcher as they used a gurney to roll me down the hall. The next thing I remembered was waking up to Detective Shapiro's hound dog grin.

"So that bait strategy with the killer, how's it working out?" he asked.

"Very effective," I said. "What do we know?"

"A man in a ski mask caught the owner of the condo directly across from yours as she was locking her car door. She gave him her keys and he locked her in the trunk. Inside her place he set up his rifle on a tripod and started shooting. He used an assault weapon, good for firing multiple rounds, causing maximum havoc, but not as precise as a sniper rifle, which would have done a lot more than wreck a quiet evening at home."

I told him how close the first few bullets passed by my head, and how he clustered the shots at where he thought I was hiding.

"He meant to put me away," I said.

I told Shapiro about his ChatJazz post and my reply.

"Were you one of those kids who teased snakes with a stick?" he asked.

"No. I've never teased anything, certainly not a snake. I love snakes."

"So you're a murder victim waiting to happen," he said. "What are we supposed to do about that?"

"Catch the guy trying to murder me."

He took a big envelope out from under his arm and pulled out a small stack of photographs. He held them out so I could see. The first was of my fancy little automatic, photographed on my kitchen counter. The next shot was a close-up of the serial number. The next a pile of shell casings and the empty clip they came from. After that, fingerprint lifts and little vials labeled "gun powder residue" and my name, and the date the samples were taken.

"You might know this gun isn't registered," he said. "Must have been an oversight."

"You know how busy people can be."

"You'll find it in your freezer. Get it done. If I don't see the paperwork in two weeks, you'll be paying Jadeen to defend an illegal possession. And by the way, no blood in the lady's apartment across the parking lot, so you missed. Tight pattern on the wall, though. Nice shooting."

They let me out three days later. Walking hurt like hell, as did sitting down and standing for more than a few minutes.

A cane helped, and it felt comforting to have a handy weapon at the ready. I convinced the condo association to let me replace the blown-out window with bullet-proof glass, a breathtaking expense even with the association picking up the cost of a standard replacement.

I checked in on ChatJazz, but there were no new posts. And I didn't leave one of my own.

I told the company I'd injured my leg, and my head, at the gym, so that was easy. It helped that the local press hadn't deemed an attempted assassination worthy of coverage. Or maybe the police beat was tied up with successful murders, which happened all too frequently in New Haven.

———— • ————

DRIVING THE Harley was another painful activity, but I drove it anyway over to meet with Erik Humboldt, who wanted to discuss his progress. When he met me at the door he asked who won the fight.

"The other guy was a barbell," I said. "There's a reason we have spotters. Good reminder for me."

He led me over to his office area which was open to most of the first-floor space. He found me a sturdy upright chair I could pull up to the desktop computer screen. Before he got started, I brought him up to speed on our recent dealings with Nelson Sarnac, leaving out certain details, but conveying the gist—that there was now a genuine, and fully informed, offer on the table that our new corporate counsel advised we seriously consider.

Erik listened to this with his vulpine grimace obscuring his reaction.

"He can certainly afford it. I'll show you, if you're up for it," he added. "You look pretty banged up."

"Thanks for that, but I'm fine."

He pulled up a spreadsheet on the computer screen that showed a list of Sarnac's interests, percentage of holdings, corporate identities, and active status. Basically, a rough map of his financial empire. He said it was still a work in progress but gave a working overview.

After taking me through the tedious analysis, he rolled back in his desk chair and swiveled around to face me. "I've got more examples, if you want to get dragged through it. Or I can just tell you the simple truth, if you want it."

"Of course. I always want the truth."

"I'd go ahead and let him buy the damn thing. You executives don't stand a chance going up against him and all that money. And even if you stop him, what do you get, except what you already have? Minus a pile of legal expenses. Negotiate big fat severances, polish up your résumés and go get other jobs that'll probably pay more, and cruise toward early retirement. Megan Rajput can go buy a villa in the south of France and staff it with hot and cold running gigolos. What the hell are you all fighting for?"

I stood up and stuffed my hands in the pockets of my jeans.

"Send me your findings, and an invoice," I said. "We're ten-day payers. And thank you. I now know what I have to do. Like my brother used to tell me, clarity is the first step toward genius."

I let myself out and rode back to New Haven. As I felt the buffeting wind in my face, the blueness began to dissipate, turning slowly into hues of red, green, and yellow.

Chapter Twenty-Four

Billy was in the office when I dropped by Los Umbros. He greeted me with his usual sloppy, XXL gusto.

"I can focus your efforts. We're looking for connections between Yolanda and Nelson Sarnac." I told him about the Young Entrepreneurs International. "I want to know what other connections exist. When and where. How close."

"What's with the cane?"

"That's the other reason I'm here."

He rousted Glen and we retired to the conference room. I asked them how much time they could give me. They said time is money, so how much money did I have. I said enough for now. Then I got more specific, asking if they could have someone keep an eye on me when I was out and about. Glen asked, reasonably, what the hell for.

"Somebody wants to kill me," I said, then described the reason for my wounded head, and limp. Preceded by the fake bomb and Wojcik's failed attack. "My only hope is to find him before he eventually pulls it off. So I can't hide. I have to live in the world. Which also means I can't go around with some entourage of meat-headed bodyguards. I need freedom of movement. What I want are guardian angels floating around my head."

Billy found this idea enjoyable, though foolhardy.

"I got people who can do this," he said, "but I'm guessing only about 50 percent likely to keep you alive. And it'll cost a bundle."

"What's a bundle?"

He gave me a number and it was a lot. But I figured Megan would happily pay it to keep her brand-new SVP available for important duties. Getting killed with a little extra money in the corporate coffers seemed like a less sensible option.

"Fine," I said. "Stick it on the tab."

———— • ————

I CAUGHT Santosan as he drove an inflatable dinghy up on the banks of Sheffield Harbor to let his dog jump out and pee. He was back in his boating outfit, which was a thread or two ahead of indecent.

"Waters," he said, slightly startled, "what the hell are you doing here?"

"I want to talk. Away from the office. Just you and me."

"There is no just you and me. I work for your company," he said.

"Did you learn to be like this at Yale, or while sucking corporate dick."

He leaned back and squinted at me, as if fearing a blow.

"What an ugly thing to say."

"I brought you into this. I trusted Jadeen to give me a lawyer with balls. What I got was a phony Mr. Miyagi who acts all wise and inscrutable, does nothing, collects a healthy fee, and goes back to his boat. Next case."

He tensed up and invaded my personal space.

"Insult is a poor way to deal with me," he said.

"I don't want to deal with you. I want you to do your damn job. What are you afraid of? Pissing off a robber baron like Nelson Sarnac? What, does he endow your university? Did he write you a check?"

The awfulness of my words seemed to strike him dumb, and immobile. His dog returned from her chores and jumped into the dinghy, barking her readiness to return to the boat.

Santosan kept his eyes locked on mine, but seemed to regain his composure, his shoulders dropping slightly, his face returning to its usual calm repose.

"What are you trying to tell me?" he asked.

"This isn't your typical suits and ties, pseudo-warfare, corporate exercise in venality and ambition. This is a real war, with headless bodies and guns, and sociopathic crimi-nals. If you don't believe me, I'll show you the bullet hole in my leg. The reason assholes like Sarnac get away with murder is assholes like you enable them. You want to just glide down from the academic heavens, dabble around, and float away. Not this time."

He reached his hand up to my face and cupped my cheek, using his thumb to brush a lock of hair out of my eyes.

"You're good at hiding your anger," he said.

"Takes practice."

"You have a lot in there."

"I've got a big fat bull's eye on my back and I'm running out of time."

He took his hand away.

"Would you like to go for a sail?"

"Sure."

After I managed to drag myself and my bum leg into the dinghy, we rode out to his sailboat. He secured it to the stern and I followed the dog up the swim ladder, though not as briskly. The dog shook out her fur, spraying me and the surrounding cockpit. Santosan told me to sit down and not move while he prepared to launch.

He started the motor, then scurried across the topsides to release the mooring line. Then he grabbed the wheel, bore off the mooring, and steered the vessel through the crowded mooring field. He edged up the throttle and had me hold the helm until we were in a narrow channel, where he gently took control, muttering something about local knowledge.

Soon after we were out on Long Island Sound. He gave me the helm so he could set the sails. It was a steadfast boat, heavy and indifferent to the chop that nagged at us as we moved away from the coast. Santosan flew around the deck like an acrobat, pulling and releasing lines and securing clutches and jam cleats, until all was in place and the boat settled into a gentle cruising posture, the point of sail just right, the angle of heel comfortable, the wheel relaxed in my hands.

I asked if he shouldn't take over.

"The machine is better at this than we are," he said, turning on the auto helm. "Let it do its job."

I sat with him in the cockpit and took in the easy rise and fall, the mingled shifts from left to right, that defined a passage over Long Island Sound in a long-keeled sailboat.

"How many people get to ride their house over the water?" he asked.

My brother and I had worked on fishing boats as summer jobs, and one year helped crew a tourist schooner that plied the waters from Eastern Long Island to the tip of Cape Cod. My brother did all the real sailing, I was more backup crew. I liked everything about it but the other people on board, who pretended to love the pitch and roll, even when they didn't, often spending hours puking in the head when they could have been breathing the sea air with me in the cockpit.

The wind shifted and the wave action intensified. Santosan got up and reset the sails, and then sat down again. I also adjusted the auto helm to better steer the boat through the waves. I knew how to do that.

"Sorry," I said to Santosan. "I should have asked. Pushing buttons was always my job."

"I don't mind if you do it properly. Which you did."

"She's a sturdy boat. Heavy displacement."

"Been around the world a half dozen times, so she ought to be."

"With you?" I asked.

"Twice."

I apologized for ripping him a new one.

"Apology accepted. Now tell me why you did it."

I wasn't sure how to answer that. Probably something to do with human brain wiring. One of my favorite professors described our rational self as Spock without a heart and our subconscious as a monkey with a gun.

"I don't like this slow march toward a sale to Nelson Sarnac," I said. "The assumption of inevitability. I agree with all the logical arguments in favor of it—I've given them myself—but it doesn't feel right. I was angry with you because I saw you as an impartial arbiter who would reveal to me what I felt but couldn't express. Instead, you joined the march."

Santosan went down into the cabin and a few minutes later asked if I wanted more of his special black tea or a beer. I yelled back that sailors who drank tea could expect to be thrown overboard. While he was away, I adjusted the auto helm again, an endless activity on the sound with its mercurial zephyrs and competing currents.

Once back in the cockpit, he apologized to me.

"We should have discussed my leanings before I announced them at the meeting. Impetuousness is one of my failings. Makes me feel like a very bad Japanese."

I accepted his apology.

"So tell me what feels wrong," he said.

I told him it was all too symmetrical: We suffer a horrible tragedy, putting the company in disarray. Sarnac offers to buy the company to put us back in order. We resist. We discover a damaging issue with the company. Sarnac goes bat shit. We resist. He comes back with a conciliatory tone, and a new offer that solves our legal problems, but at a greatly reduced price. All the stars are now aligned, and the owner's hand is being drawn toward the sales agreement like a compass to magnetic north.

Meanwhile, I'm over in a dark corner fighting off this malevolent force that could be just out to get me, or maybe, part of the greater story.

"There's plenty of science that tells us our instincts are often smarter than we are. When my gut tells me something is wrong, it's usually right, even if I can't give you a rational argument."

He gave a little bow. I bowed back.

"I promise I will become a skeptic and dig deeper," he said.

"Thank you."

"Drink your beer, I got more below."

We sailed for a while, then brought the boat about, turning through the wind and letting it push us back to home port. The current was now in our favor, so the trip was the equivalent of peddling up a hill, then cruising down the other side. The wind noise also subsided, letting me hear the slap of the waves against the hull and the flap of the sails overhead grabbing and letting go of the wind.

Further business talk was forsworn, and we sailed in silence back to the mouth of Sheffield Harbor, where he kicked over the engine and we motored to his mooring. The dog urged us to promptly deploy the dinghy and head to shore, where we all pissed in the reedy grass, and I took my leave. Santosan let me go with little ceremony, and before I knew it, I was piloting my Harley Sportster over terra firma, where any clumsy dips and shoves right or left were my responsibility, not the result of the restless, uncontrollable sea.

Megan Rajput brought me into her office and asked if I could have dinner at her house. I said that was a bad idea. She straightened her shoulders and locked my eyes before saying, "I've been an asshole to you, while you've been a perfect gentleman with me. I'm sorry. I want to make it up to you, but more importantly, I just want to talk. You and me without all these other people hanging around."

I told her she wasn't an asshole. In fact, she'd been pretty heroic through it all. I was flattered that she might want to get intimate, but I thought things were confused enough without throwing that into the mix. Not that I didn't think she was beautiful and desirable, and great company.

"I used to be great company," she said. "Back when I could let all the Irish out."

"There's still plenty of Irish in there, it just has a different agenda."

"I can't cook for shit, so I have a husband and wife team who do all the cooking, serving, and cleaning up. They can chaperone."

"No swimming," I said.

"No swimming."

It looked like all the available outside lights were lit at Megan's house. I parked the Harley next to an old Nissan van and rang the bell. She answered the door wearing black pants and a loose sweater over a silk dark blue T-shirt. I handed her a bottle of wine.

"I asked for red," I said. "This is what they gave me."

"Well done."

She led me into a small study. A woman in a white shirt and black skirt followed us with two small plates of finger food.

Megan gave her my wine offering, and I told the woman any beer was good enough. We sat in two big club chairs facing the fireplace, fireless as appropriate to the summer season.

"I guess having help is sort of elitist, but all that messing around in the kitchen and cleaning up," she said, "can't be bothered."

"I'm sure they appreciate the work."

She sighed as if reluctantly giving in to the inevitable.

"I'm glad you came, Waters," she said, as we got comfortable. "I appreciate it. How's the leg?"

"Much better, thanks. Don't need the cane."

"You gotta stop getting so banged around."

"I'm working on that."

She told me that her father lifted weights as part of his training as an amateur boxer. He also ran, did pushups, and jumped rope. By the time she was old enough to understand why he did these things, he was aging out of the sport. His day job was working as a stevedore on the docks in Long Island City, another fading profession, but he made it to retirement before the work dried up, a blessing, she said. She had a childhood as pampered and privileged as any Upper East Side princess, in that she never wanted for anything, and never felt threatened or alone. In retrospect, her father was clearly a feared man, and there were three older brothers more than capable of keeping her secure when he wasn't around.

Since her mother had died when she was two years old, this was all the family she had.

The family's project was to get her through high school and into a good college, which she did, first Hofstra, then earning an MBA in finance at NYU. The first in her family to make it past ninth grade. The deal she made in her own mind, never shared with anyone, was to do what they wanted, but have her own life off hours.

"I was the wildest bookworm in New York City."

It helped that the few times she got into trouble she could call her brothers, and all would be made right, in short order. This was a shameful thing, she now thought, but was still grateful, and wrote it off as the stupid stuff all young people do.

Her greatest regret was hiding her relationship with Paresh, whom she met in New Haven while working at an accounting firm that gave pro bono advice to young entrepreneurs. She lost twenty pounds and nearly became addicted to Xanax trying to keep it secret, until it just became too much and she broke down in the middle of Thanksgiving dinner and spilled her guts, not just metaphorically, all over a table filled with turkey, cranberry sauce, and mashed potatoes.

Her father cleaned her up and told her he could give two shits that Paresh was Hindu, telling her that the Irish and Indians had both been ruled over by the fucking Limeys, and so they were brothers under the skin, and all that mattered

to him was that Paresh was a stand-up guy and would take
good care of her.

She told him Paresh was a stand-up guy.

"That's good enough."

I asked her how Paresh got along with them.

"They all got drunk together one night, and when he
woke them up the next morning with some stinky Indian
hangover cure, that actually worked, he was in. Paresh could
charm the stripes off an angry tiger. His quote, not mine."

We talked some more, then she asked to be excused so
she could dress more like a hostess, and I said of course.

"They have a nice dinner waiting near the pool."

While she was away, I wandered around the house, perplexed as always with what people did with all that space.
Vast expanses were dedicated to the placement of objects
and redundant seating options. Or just plain empty space,
usually between functional areas, like the kitchen and dining
room, living room and den. I understood it was all nice to
look at, but once you looked at it, then what?

To be fair to Megan, she used to share all that space with
another person. I wondered if she was considering a smaller
house but didn't know a diplomatic way to ask.

The husband half of the dinner team was orchestrating
a stove full of steaming and crackling pots and pans. Serving dishes and small and large plates were arrayed on the
counters and center island. He looked annoyed to see me
drift into his domain, scooping the presentation to come. I
backed away with an apology.

Megan appeared wearing a floor-length skirt and silk
blouse and we started the long journey out to the patio. I
told her I was impressed by the roominess of her home, as
with the aesthetics, not what you'd expect looking from the
street.

"That was another compromise with Paresh," she said. "He wanted a smaller house until he saw how big a basement you could get with an oversized ranch."

"His shop?"

She laughed.

"You could call it that. Want to see?"

"Okay."

The stairwell was behind a door in a utility room next to the garage. She flicked on the light and we walked down steps made of one-and-one-half-inch slabs of hardwood.

"Before we moved in, he raised the ceiling a few feet, or rather, sunk the floor."

At the bottom of the stairs I turned left and looked out at a fully equipped prototyping facility. Long metal benches covered in semi-assembled components, bulky CAD/CAM machines of every size and purpose, 3D printers, laser cutters, material stock and bins full of mechanical and electronic parts stacked on rolling racks, electronics lab, testing booths, micro-machining tools, ovens, a ratty old-fashioned drawing table, brilliant LED lighting, an epoxy-painted floor, a yoga mat, and everything else we had back at ExciteAble's R&D lab.

"I called it Rajput World," she said. "He never let me sell tickets."

She brought me over to an alcove with a single bed, night table, two large cabinets, a kitchenette with a sink, microwave, and full-sized refrigerator, and a full bath.

"This is where he usually slept," she said. "Said he didn't want to wake me up, but I knew he was afraid to miss an alarm from the test benches that might wreck a project. Or maybe he couldn't find our bedroom in the dark."

I only half-heard her as I struggled to absorb what I was seeing, and what it was telling me.

"This is where ExciteAble's prototypes were actually made," I said. "The lab at the company just finished them off."

Megan clinked her wine glass with my beer.

"Not that they knew," she said.

She pulled me by the shirtsleeve over to a test bench where an electronic device was hooked up to an array of diagnostic equipment. It looked like a premature black box on life support.

"His last work in progress," she said.

"What does it do?"

"Anything you want. Theoretically."

"Make an omelet?" I asked.

"Sure, if you're making it on an aircraft." She walked over to the device on which she rested her hand as if checking its temperature. She switched her wine to her left hand and used her right to slide a keyboard out from under the bench, then tapped out something on the keys. Columns of numbers popped up on a screen mounted among the jangle of displays above the device. She scrolled down, stopped and looked, then scrolled down again. Then she handed me her wine and used both hands to write a string of code into the system. She hit enter and watched the columns reconfigure. She studied them for a moment, then used her hip to bump the keyboard back under the bench.

"Sad," she said.

"What is?"

"He never got it to work."

She grabbed my sleeve and pulled me back toward the stairs. I put up a little resistance and she let go. "Come on, our dinner is probably cooling off out on the patio."

The husband and wife stood at attention to either side of a table covered in a white tablecloth. As soon as we sat down, a first course was in front of us. I didn't know what it was, but there was meat involved with an edible garnish, and it tasted great. Megan asked me about my first dog, a subject I always found entrancing, despite her tragic end, and Megan painted a moving portrait of a Siamese cat she rescued from the streets of Brooklyn, and so the conversation went.

The following courses were equally delicious, and the subject matter pleasantly banal, punctuated by moments of humor that got us both laughing like loons.

After one of these moments, she wiped her eye with a napkin and said, "I'm going to miss you, Waters."

That caught me unawares.

"I'm not planning to go anywhere."

"You will. The good ones always do. That's okay. I already forgive you."

I heard a man yell something off in the woods behind the house. Another angry bee passed over my head. I shoved the table into Megan, pushing her backward off her chair. She looked at me with wild eyes and screamed. Another scream came from a few feet away. More rounds followed as I yanked the little table clear and lay on top of her. Someone yelled something in the near distance. I grabbed Megan by the front of her nice blouse and dragged her behind a cluster of potted hibiscus. One of the pots thudded back into us, clay spraying out across the patio. I heard the woman server whimper in Spanish.

I retrieved the automatic from my rear waistband and used my other hand to gather the big potted plants into a semicircle between us and the incoming fire. I wrapped my body around Megan and said, "Just stay still. You'll be fine."

Silence followed, a long silence filled only with Megan's breathing and the Spanish entreaties of the server lady. I told Megan to stay where she was and crawled over to the other woman. Her upper left shoulder was a sea of dark red. I ripped open the shirt and saw the bullet hole, bleeding, but not gushing. Her husband came in a frantic crabwalk across the patio. I told him to press firmly into the wound.

They were both crying but did what I said.

Lying on my back, I pulled out my phone and called 911.

When I was sure the dispatcher got the message, I checked on the husband and wife. Her blood was everywhere, but her eyes looked alert, her forehead warm. I ripped a big piece of fabric off my shirt and balled it up, handing it to the husband, who stuck it between his hand and the wound. I rolled over to where Megan was lying immobile behind the big pots and grabbed her by the waist.

"How's the girl?" she asked.

"Could be worse. How are you?"

"Terrified."

"You throw a hell of a dinner party."

I heard another yell coming from a stand of trees behind the house. We both stayed still and listened. Then another yell.

"Did you hear what he said?" I asked her.

"I think 'All clear.'"

"All clear?"

I listened as hard as I could, until hearing the sound of rustling leaves, heading our way. I moved off Megan and aimed the automatic in that direction.

"Close enough," I yelled.

"Don't shoot," a man said. "I'm with Billy."

"Keep your hands in the air," I said.

"Already doing that. In fact, I'm lying down right where I am. Maybe take a little nap."

Lights flickered in the treetops. Red and blue. An amplified voice commanded everyone to stay in place.

Megan pressed into me from behind, wiggling against my rear end.

"You're a good protector," she said. "I'm glad you're still alive."

Flashlights crisscrossed over our heads. The cop with the bullhorn repeated the demand that everyone stay in place, hands where they could see them. I had Megan call out our position, assuming a female voice would draw a quicker, less trigger-happy response. Moments later, we were bathed in light and surrounded by police.

"There's a guy in the woods," I said. "Lying in the leaves. I think he's on our side. Please don't shoot him."

They let us stand up, and I was grateful not to be frisked, given the burning ache coming from my leg wound, yet to be fully felt. I gave them an accounting of what happened, interrupted by the arrival of a pack of cops and a young man with a shaved head, wearing fatigues and a black T-shirt. He held a wad of gauze up to the side of his face.

"Sorry I couldn't hold on to him," the guy said. "But I guess he missed."

He said he was leaning against a tree watching us eat dinner when he saw movement barely twenty feet in front of him. When he saw the shape of a rifle, he ran toward the shooter, shouted "Hey," then dropped to the ground. He heard a shot. The shooter got off a few more rounds in our direction before the young man got back on his feet, ran over, and leaped on his back.

"The son of a bitch flipped me off like a bug and gun-butted my face."

"That was incredibly brave," said Megan.

"Incredibly stupid," he said. "I should've just shot him. But you were in my line of fire, and my night vision was all messed up from staring at your house."

He introduced himself as an off-duty police officer sent to keep an eye on me. One of the cops handed him a fresh pad of gauze and said he needed to sit down and wait for the paramedics. I walked over to where two others were administering to the wounded woman and asked how she was doing. They said not bad but would surely love for the ambulance to show up.

I called Detective Shapiro and told him what happened. He asked me to give the phone to one of the officers and they spoke for a while. Another cop was using a Sharpie to draw a circle on the kitchen wall. Billy's guy was also on his cell phone. When he hung up, he said another of the team would come over and stay that night with Mrs. Rajput. I thanked him and asked if there was anything he could tell me about the shooter.

"Trained. Fast and strong. Didn't see his face. Dressed in black, black knit cap. Sorry, that's all I can tell you. I think I passed out for a second when he slugged me. I don't know why he didn't stick a bullet in my head. Could've."

Unnecessary, I thought. Not merciful, just a bloodless decision.

The new guy from Los Umbros showed up and Megan gave him a tour of the house. An hour later all but two of the cops left, telling her the CSIs would be showing up any minute. They also left a patrolman in the driveway. With all that, she said I should go home and get some sleep.

Which I did, though I admit to a few nerves on the ride from her house. I always had a terrible time with arithmetic, but I could add, and understood the basic laws of probability. With each assault on my life, the killer was getting closer. By my reckoning, we were now down to inches.

And the game was clearly coming to an end.

CHAPTER TWENTY-FIVE

I hate to lie in bed after waking in the morning. I find the confusing admixture of dreams and real life disturbing, and if I let it linger too long, it will infect my whole day. So I tend to bound up at the moment of consciousness, a practice that has cost me more than one potential life partner.

The morning after the night at Megan's began the usual way, not realizing that the bullet wound in my thigh had been sorely tested by the evening's acrobatics, which also spawned a fresh array of injury and abuse, such that I fell to the floor as quickly as I rose from the bed.

Lying there, my face raw from rug burn, I had a new thought. I cupped that thought in the mental palm of my hand, like a newborn desperate to catch its first breath.

The name Gestalt popped into my head.

I found the study of psychology to be an exercise in explaining why all the great contributors to the field were basically wrong. We still had to learn what their principles were, so we could pass the exams and advance toward the degree. This seemed ridiculous to me. If the professors thought famous psychologists were all wrong, why the hell learn their principles? Doesn't that belong in the history department?

In the end, I felt lucky that I absorbed all that information, because I concluded that none of the great thinkers were exactly wrong, they just had a partial hold on the truth. Take the Gestalt theorists. They believed that people were capable of perceiving a whole that was more meaningful than the sum of its constituent parts. I never saw a problem with that. My brother said it was like appreciating a car engine purring away without having to ponder the interaction among ignition, carburetor, cylinders, and valves.

Individual stitches that only express themselves in whole cloth.

I flipped over onto my back and looked at the ceiling, seeing for the first time a scar in the plaster that led to a dent in the base of the ceiling fan. A bullet track, revealed through a change in perspective.

I went over to the desktop and logged onto ChatJazz. No new posts from Plato. I posted my own message:

"Wrong. You're dead."

I went to work and checked in with Joey Adams. He looked exhausted and was nearly vibrating with nervous energy. The first thing he did was apologize for letting my mail pile up in the mail room and forgetting to water the plants in the reception area. I told him we'd reassign those tasks, and any other administrative grunt work he used to command.

"Make a list," I said.

"Thanks, chief. I have another list of stuff only you can do, and don't even tell me I can do them, because I can't." He dug around a file he was holding and handed me some printouts. "And who's the muscly guy she's got with her? Bodyguard?"

"Beefed-up security. I'll explain later. Nothing to worry about."

"I don't exactly believe you, but that's okay. I'm too busy to worry about anything but getting through all this work. Let me know if a nuclear holocaust is coming. I can at least take a moment to kiss my ass good-bye."

I went to Megan's office and found the aforementioned bodyguard sitting at an admin's desk outside her door. He was pecking away at his own laptop, the admin's keyboard shoved into a corner of the desk.

I introduced myself, and he cordially shook my hand, saying it was always a pleasure to meet the people paying the bills. Then he let Megan know I was there, and she let me in.

"I feel like I was hit by a truck," she said. "How about you?"

"Likewise. Better than getting hit by an assault rifle." We both sat slowly in our chairs, smiling at the shared experience. "Hey, Megan, the whole time last night I was meaning to ask you about Sarnac. Do you mind talking about it now?"

She seemed fine with that.

"Sure. What do you want to know?"

"His offer. What's your current thinking, if you don't mind me asking."

She folded her arms across her chest and took a deep breath.

"I'm thinking of saying yes. Before you start in on me, I want you to know that last night put me over the edge. I can't take it anymore. I'm only forty-two years old. I got a lot of life in front of me. I'm not ready to die of stress, or overwork, or a bullet through my head right when I'm about to take a sip of tasty red wine. I could spend the next few years doing nothing but fight the man, who will likely win and shut us down, wiping out everything I have. Instead, Sarnac will write a check that takes the financial thing right off the table. I can move to the south of France. Hire people to cook breakfast and drive me around in big, black cars. Go to the casino, buy friends and order up hot and cold running gigolos. What kind of idiot wouldn't take a deal like that? And by the way, I like you a lot, Waters, but you're not getting another dinner invitation."

"Who said I'd accept?"

She tore a piece of paper off a small pad, crumpled it up, and threw it at me.

"Do you agree or not?" she said.

"Okay by me. Do you want Santosan to handle the negotiations?"

"Absolutely. Love that little guy."

I stood up and reached across the desk. She took my hand.

"You might consider relocating yourself," she said. "This town seems to be bad for your health."

"Noted."

I sat down at my desk at the office and made two phone calls. In both cases, I hit voice mail, which was fine with me. The first to Santosan, telling him Megan wanted to go ahead with the sale to Sarnac. This was the official call to trigger negotiations, though I hoped he would keep our conversation in mind as he went through the process.

The next was to thank Los Umbros for saving my life, and Megan Rajput's in the bargain, and to ask for an update on their work on Yolanda Alexander.

A few hours later Billy at Los Umbros called to say they had some interesting things to share, if I could come on by at the end of the day. I said sure.

Billy and Glen were both out in the waiting room when I got there. I took the chance to thank them again for saving my ass, and they tried to modestly deflect the appreciation. I asked how the hero of the night was doing with the wound to his face, and they said ten stitches and a Percodan and he was back on the job in the morning.

Billy's wife was in the conference room with a cooler full of beer and a big basket of hard pretzels.

"We do this every night at closing time," said Glen.

"So don't start feeling honored," said Billy.

After cracking the beers, Glen stood up at an easel and turned over the big chart paper. On the left column was four of Yolanda's many professional assignments, with the company names and dates of service. On the right were the companies' connections to Nelson Sarnac, with Yolanda's operational proximity. They didn't have to tally it all up.

"She knew him for years," I said.

"Oh, yeah," said Glen. "She had a web-based service that sent out her Christmas cards. He'd been on her list for a while. Don't ask me how I know that."

"Okay, we know Yolanda knew Sarnac," I said. "How does that fit into the larger theory?"

Glen shot a look at his brother, reluctant to take the stage, but Billy waved him on.

"I'm more comfortable talking about facts than spinning fairy tales, but since you asked, I think Sarnac has a serious hard-on for ExciteAble Technologies," he said. "The guy's old, he hears the clock ticking. He's looking for a big score as if it can delay the big sleep. He doesn't have anything else to do. No family, no big cause to speak of, just a hunger for one more home run. We deal with these kinds of guys all the time. Mostly marital crap, where the wife's lawyer hires us to tell her the obvious, that the bastard's got some chippie in an apartment in Midtown. None of that here."

"Tell him about the other guy," said Billy. "Erik Humboldt."

"Not much more to tell. He specializes in white collar crime. Has mostly corporate clients, though he consults with government prosecutors, state and federal. People say he's very good at what he does. Went to night school while working as a cop in New York City, earned his CPA and Series 7 stockbroker's license. Except for that deadly force event, never been in a lick of trouble."

I thanked them for the information and they asked what I wanted them to do next. I said to sit tight on research and focus on keeping me alive. And Megan Paresh.

"Record her comings and goings," I said. "The killer will be looking for patterns he can exploit."

"Got it."

I was almost out the door when I remembered something else.

"Colin Brice?" I asked them. "Got anything?"

Glen disappeared into his office and came back with a manila envelope. He handed it to me.

"Let me know if you want more," he said.

"Headline?"

"A true Boy Scout. Ex-military, big in community activities, healthy marriage, no record, not even a traffic ticket."

"I figured that," I said.

"Spent ten years as a forensic accountant for the State Police. Did that come up in his job interview?"

"No. It didn't."

CHAPTER TWENTY-SIX

I was taking a shower and listening to the radio when I heard on the business news that ExciteAble Technologies had accepted a takeover bid by Sarnac Enterprises worth eighty million dollars in cash and Sarnac stock, a sixty-million-dollar haircut from the original offer.

There wasn't much more than a brief statement by Sarnac that this acquisition had terrific synergies benefitting all and promised to bring new jobs and expanded opportunity to the state of Connecticut.

I took longer getting ready for work, so it was well after the usual start time that I got there and waved at Joey Adams to follow me into my office.

"I knew something was cooking," he said, closing my office door behind him.

"Is Megan here?"

"In her office with Colin and Fred Warner. Hasn't asked for you."

"What's the mood of the troops?"

"Nervous. People hate change. People also hate getting news sprung on them, so they're sort of pissed. All the little gossipy birdies have been all over me."

"You don't know anything," I said.

"That's what I keep telling them, since actually, I don't. Megan's called a company meeting for three o'clock. So maybe we'll learn something then."

He was pacing around my office, so I asked him to have a seat. He obliged.

"I wasn't sure this was coming, but I thought it might," I said. "And I'm not sure if it's good or bad for the company, or which of us will be affected one way or the other, including you. If and when I get some clarity, you'll be the first to know."

He looked down at his lap and nodded.

"I know. You've always been square with me. When you can."

"Just keep doing what you're doing. Your instincts are excellent. You'll be fine."

He looked up again.

"My instincts are telling me you won't be around much," he said. "What do I say to people who ask about that?"

"You'll know."

I parked myself outside Megan's office in a sofa opposite her admin's desk, still occupied by the Los Umbros bodyguard. He was fine with that, and seemed to be happily occupied with his iPhone, a copy of the *New York Post* and the admin's desktop computer, on which he was doing who-knows-what. He was a very bulky person, exaggerated maybe by his loose-fitting suit jacket and bigger-than-normal bald head. He wore what would have been called a goatee, but for the hair extending from ear to chin in a thin, straight line.

His other pastime was eating something from a rumpled paper bag. I never saw what it was, though you could hear the crunch from a few yards away. The employees working nearby thought better than to complain.

Eventually the office door opened, and Colin and Fred Warner walked out. They didn't seem disturbed to see me sitting there, though their greetings were brief and perfunctory. Megan stood leaning on the door jamb and waved me in.

"You think I'm a coward," she said, sweeping across the floor and dropping into the chair behind her desk.

"I don't. I think you're doing the right thing."

"A coward for not telling you ahead of time."

I swatted that thought with the back of my hand, like you'd return the lob of a beach ball.

"I always said it was your call. You don't owe me any special notice."

She crinkled her nose at me.

"So you're okay with it," she said, in a voice high enough to be dangerously close to infantile.

"Completely okay. Happy for you."

"Even after you saved my life."

"Listen, Megan. This nutjob is my problem, not yours. I almost got you killed going over there for dinner. It's got nothing to do with the company. The bodyguard outside is a precaution. Let's just move on and let you deal with the sale and let me deal with my own crap."

"That sounds like you're quitting."

"I can if you want, or I can help with the transition. It's up to you. But I'm not working for Nelson Sarnac. I agree with you on the cigars. They're a nonstarter."

She stood up and went around the desk. I stayed seated. She sat on the armrest of my chair and put her arm around my shoulder.

"I'll never stop appreciating everything you did for me," she said.

"I'm sure that's true. And vice versa."

She squeezed my shoulder and moved her hand down the back of my arm, squeezing along the way.

"There's more to you than meets the eye," she said.

I held her gaze.

"Just don't look too closely."

I was driving my car back to the condo when a call came in from Olivia Lefèvre. She was whispering.

"Waters. Help me."

I pulled off the road.

"What's going on?"

"It's the first chance I've had to call. We're at a bar. I snatched this poor girl's phone. I'm in the ladies' room. He's right outside. There's a band playing, do you hear it?" I said I did. "I texted you the GPS coordinates of where he's keeping me. Please come. Don't tell anyone. He owns the cops up here. They'll give me up. Please, just come." I heard banging. "Oh, God," she murmured, then yelled, "I'm sick, Erik. Just give me a couple minutes."

The last thing I heard her whisper was, "Please."

Billy and I ran through the coordinates a half dozen times and kept coming up with the same location—the top of a mountain on the border of Vermont and Northwest Massachusetts, equally inaccessible from everywhere. I searched around the Internet for advice on the best way to penetrate the forest—how close you could get with a vehicle, before resorting to trails. What kind of terrain we could expect. There wasn't much because few ever troubled to go there.

Billy called a hunter friend who had the best counsel, and better yet, a map showing trails and hazards, which he scanned and sent over. I lined it up with Google Earth and an old topographical. An hour later we had a plan of approach.

"How do you feel about hiking?" I asked Billy.

"Fine. Walk all over hell and gone hunting deer. Not a fast walker, but I never slow down. Glen calls me the energizer bunny. Camos, good boots, rain parka. I'm good for at least forty-eight hours straight if I can nap an hour every twelve. Oh, and a Ruger deer rifle with a custom sight and synthetic stock."

We talked more about gear, what we could pool and what to buy. The idea was to bring only essentials to reduce weight, the trick knowing what was essential and what wasn't.

"And only what we need to go in, not to get out," I said. "We find her, we take her, we call in the helicopters."

"Got it."

I bought two used trail bikes on the way to my condo. I crammed one in the back seat of my car and strapped the other to the roof. Billy was to pick me up in his truck the next day before dawn. Before going to bed, I spent some time going through my Great Escape equipment—assessing, then keeping or rejecting each item. I'd wear a set of Billy's camos. I had my own rugged, lightweight boots. He had a sealed pack of energy bars that we could live on for two days, I brought a small first-aid kit that included breathable adhesive patches, sewing kit, and a pre-filled syringe of morphine. And a pair of walkie-talkies with in-ear headsets similar to smartphone ear buds.

More important than any of this was my handheld GPS in the rugged case, with a night-vision screen and a week's worth of battery power.

Billy arrived in his pickup with a tray of bad coffee purchased at the gas station where he filled up. I drank it anyway. We put the trail bikes in the truck bed and drove more than three hours of interstate and two-lane, twisty roads through the Berkshires, until we hit the first dirt road. According to the map, a four-wheel vehicle could take that road about twenty miles into the woods before running out of clear passage. From there, trail bikes could go another ten miles before the trail petered out, at which time, the only way through was on foot.

This is when Billy asked if I had a plan.

"We get to within a few hundred feet of the location while it's still daylight," I said. "Then we lie on our backs and figure out what to do next."

"Since it all depends on what we find there," he said.

"That's right. No point in speculating now."

"Okay, let's roll."

———— • ————

THE DIRT road was remarkably similar to the one that led into the woods behind my childhood home. More pines and conifers, and sharp rocks protruding up from the road bed, but equally dense and flush with varied plant life, tall and proud or rotting on the ground.

The road ended with a finality that wasn't apparent on the map. A natural barricade of felled trees blocked further passage, though a bike path, clearly visible, curved around the debris. We parked the truck where others had obviously parked before.

"You didn't ask me how good I was with a mountain bike," said Billy.

"How good are you?"

"Iffy."

"So you lead. I'll leave enough space so if you fall down I won't run over you."

We rode around the small clearing getting used to the bikes' handling and gearing before Billy felt confident enough to launch down the trail. Despite the disclaimers, he moved along with precision and self-assurance, if not speed, a graceful athlete disguised by his hulking frame.

True to the map, a defined trail eventually turned into undifferentiated forest and undergrowth. I kept up with his try at navigating the chaos, with some struggle, until the inevitable clawed us both to the ground. He was laughing as he went down.

"Freaking hell," he said, prone and half under the bike. "That's a workout."

I lay a few feet behind catching my breath and pulled out the GPS. We'd gone a little off course, but still mostly on track. I crawled up to him and set another course, taking small hills and dense open fields into account, and shared my thinking. It made sense to him.

"We have to consider security cams and motion detectors," he said. "Could really mess with the element of surprise."

This was all I'd been thinking about for the last few hours, so I gave him my conclusions.

"We get to within about four hundred yards of the location, and split up," I said. "According to this topographical," I showed him the map, "there's a little rise next to the location. You go there and set up a sniper position, hopefully with a view of the front door, assuming the building has a front door. I'll get close and set these off outside the house," I showed him a handful of cherry bombs, "to draw and hold his attention. Then I go through the back and shoot everybody but Olivia. God willing."

"What am I supposed to do?"

"Shoot any male who isn't me. In the legs, which we might be able to fix well enough to keep them alive."

"That's not a very sophisticated plan," he said.

"You have a better one?"

"No."

"So?"

"Let's do it."

We thrashed our way forward for another two hours before getting within visual distance of the location. We rested for a few moments, drank some water and ate energy bars, then took two different routes, me toward the location, Billy toward the small hill. We tested the walkie-talkies as we moved through the woods.

"He could be watching us now on infrared," said Billy.

"A meteor could be about to crash into the earth, destroying all life as we know it."

"Thanks for that. Makes me feel better."

It was a Quonset hut. I estimated about ten feet wide and twice that in length. In the fading daylight I could see a satellite dish, a wood pile and scattered branches and wood chips surrounding a thick slice of tree trunk used to help split the firewood.

"You see it?" I whispered to Billy.

"Yep. Got a good sight line front and back."

"Is there a back door?" I asked.

"There is."

I took a deep breath, lit the cherry bombs, and heaved them toward the front of the Quonset hut. Having been lit in quick succession, they exploded in the same order, pop, pop, pop.

As I ran around to the other end, Billy fired a half-dozen rounds through the top of the hut, with any luck, high enough to avoid the people inside. Since I was already running, I made a wide curve so I could head straight into the door. It wasn't a brilliant concept but had the charm of simplicity. I'd never understood physics, but I'd heard that things get more massive the faster they traveled, thus more powerful. I felt I was already a pretty massive person, so the faster I ran, the more energy would be hitting that door.

Turns out I was right, though the door itself had some physical properties of its own. I busted through, but not without rattling my teeth and blurring my vision.

Erik was on the floor with his arm around Olivia, who lay next to him. They were facing the opposite direction, which was my hope. I only had a few seconds to clear my head, just in time to see Erik roll over on his back and start to lift a big .45-caliber handgun. I shot over his head and yelled, "Drop it!"

His gun was maybe six inches off the floor, aimed at my shins, but my little automatic was aimed at his head. Olivia squirmed out of his grasp and scrambled toward me. Quick as a mongoose, Erik sat up and grabbed her by the ankle, yanking hard. She screamed and went down like a felled tree, smacking her head on the floor. He leaned forward and grabbed her by the butt, sliding her back in his direction. He stood up and dragged her to her feet, gathering up a handful of her hair and sticking the .45 hard against her cheek.

"What are you doing?" he yelled at Olivia.

"Let her go," I said. "You're done. Killing her doesn't achieve anything."

"He killed Rajput," she said to me. "And tried to frame you. And when that didn't work, tried to wreck your career, and then kill you. He knew about us from the beginning. I'm so stupid. He's a fucking psychopath, Waters. I'm so sorry. It's all my fault."

He looked down at her, puzzled.

"What are you saying?"

He used the hand without a gun to stroke her cheek. She shook it off.

"He thinks I'm his possession," said Olivia. "That I violated his trust when I let you violate me. He vowed to make your life a living hell. That's what he's done to mine."

Erik looked up at me and chuckled.

"Do you believe this woman? After all I did for her?"

"Let her go," I repeated.

"I hate you," said Olivia. "I will hate you for the rest of my life."

He looked puzzled.

"I'm not getting this," he said.

"You disgust me. Get it over with. Pull the trigger."

Erik was a tough read, but I think I saw something like astonishment, blended with fury.

"You fucking bitch," he said, pulling her head back and shoving the .45 deeper into her face.

I heard a burst of gunfire behind me, a rapid pattern from a heavy handgun. Erik was thrown back, his face filled with bewilderment, his chest full of holes.

Chapter Twenty-Seven

As I suspected, the only way in or out of there was on foot or by helicopter. Erik had used a New Haven taxi chopper to deliver him and Olivia; we got the services of the Massachusetts State Police.

Olivia told us voice calls wouldn't go through, but we could text 911 with our GPS coordinates, which would bypass the local cops and go directly to the staties, the only ones who could afford air support. The helicopter disgorged a half-dozen cops in full SWAT regalia. All three of us stood under the brilliant ground lights with our hands behind our heads, guns at our feet. Two of the cops patted us down while the rest entered the building like the team of commandos they were.

They also frisked Olivia, apologizing through most of it. She said, just do your jobs and don't worry about it. As they looked at our IDs and wrote in little case books, Billy told them we'd left a number of items on a table that could be material evidence in ongoing murder investigations. He said they were found in plain sight and we hadn't touched anything else, which fingerprints and DNA will prove. We just wanted to be sure those things were set aside.

"Don't touch anything till you glove up," he yelled to the cops in the hut.

Included in a little collection on the table was a Homer Simpson mask and a hand-held monitor used with GPS trackers.

I gave one of the cops Detective Shapiro's cell number and asked if he could give the detective a call. And if it was okay, if I could talk to him too. He said he'd ask the sergeant. It wasn't long before they secured the scene and told us to climb aboard the chopper for the trip to the barracks where they'd take our statements. That's where I got to talk to Shapiro on the phone, who gave me a load of crap for not disclosing Olivia's situation, but I charmed him by describing all the evidence we found at Erik Humboldt's hut. I stood with my arm over Olivia's shoulder throughout the call. She had both her arms around me. When I hung up, I asked how she was doing, since every once in a while, a tremor seemed to pass through her body.

"I always shake a little after someone tries to kill me. I'll work on that."

They took our statements separately but seemed satisfied enough to let us go just as the sun was coming up. They dropped Olivia and me off at a motel, but Billy wanted to retrieve his truck, so he left promising to come back and take us home.

Olivia and I managed to reacquaint ourselves with the more intimate aspects of the relationship before falling asleep, and awakened when Billy showed up a few hours later.

When we reached my condo, I grabbed my car and drove Olivia to her house in Westbrook. Only then did she start talking about fleeing New York the night Erik showed up at our restaurant, stopping at her house to grab some essentials, and almost making it out the driveway before he blocked her with the Jag, and forced her at gunpoint back into the house. From there it was a blur of locked closets, nights handcuffed to the bed, trips in the car when she tried to leap out only to learn that the Jaguar automatically locked the doors as soon as the car started to move, and Erik had disabled her controls.

She couldn't get a voice message to me until she scooped a woman's phone off a lunch counter and convinced Erik that she was in desperate need of a bathroom. Then she called me.

"You surprised him, Waters," she said, describing what he'd told her at the cabin. "The plan was to throw you into abject terror, torture you until you couldn't take it anymore, then kill you. Instead, the harder he went at you, the harder you came back. You were wily, unpredictable. You hired him, for Chrissakes." She laughed. "Totally threw him for a loop. I knew he'd underestimate you, but of course, he didn't ask me. Why would he? Master detective and all that. I could have told him you were different from the corporate weasels he usually dealt with. Not that I would. It was too much fun watching him thrash around in frustration."

"I'm just glad he didn't hurt you. The fear never went away."

She rubbed the top of my thigh.

"Now the fear's gone forever, Waters. You have no idea how wonderful that feels."

During the time since her rescue she seemed jittery and enervated, but fundamentally stable, in possession of herself. But when we walked into her house in Westbrook, she went over to the living room sofa, curled in a ball and wept like she'd lost every friend she ever had. I sat next to her and stroked her hair, waiting it out.

"I'll never forget what you did for me, Waters," she said in a tear-soaked voice. "Or forgive myself for what I did to you."

"It wasn't your fault. Quit with all that."

She squeezed my hand and sighed. Soon after she was asleep, the trembles finally subsided. I sat there and watched her sleep until a shot of sun from a big window on the east side of the house woke her up.

Her eyes flicked open and she smiled at me.

Detective Shapiro brought Andy Pettigrew along for our interviews. We were also joined by Jadeen Knox and a Massachusetts State Police detective. Olivia had already done her bit, I was next, and Billy would be last. Jadeen sat in with Olivia, at my request, and would also stay for Billy's. It all seemed natural for everyone involved, especially given the pro forma nature of the exercise.

Shapiro went through the facts of the matter, having me confirm and clarify. The Massachusetts detective had his own questions, many dealing with our decision not to involve the local police. I told him Olivia expressly warned us to keep them out of the loop, and I didn't think it was worth the risk to ignore her. Our best hope was the element of surprise, which probably resulted in a successful outcome, with only the perpetrator losing his life.

The detective told Shapiro and Jadeen that he'd asked all his questions, offering no opinion of my answers, but his manner suggested he was satisfied. After that, Shapiro got more subjective.

"If it's okay with you, Dr. Waters, I wonder if you could give your professional opinion on Erik Humboldt's state of mind. Andy, chime in if you want."

I'd obviously thought about this a lot, so I was ready with an answer.

"Without getting too clinical," I said, "he had an extreme form of narcissism, the type that presents as an exaggerated sense of dominance over intimate relationships. Note I didn't say people he loves, because it may not be love. It's more that he has something no one else is allowed to have. Possessiveness on steroids. We had a dog when I was a kid who felt that way about a certain green ball. Slept with it, carried it around in her mouth, would fight another dog to the death to hold on to it. If you said there's a strong element of obsessive-compulsive in that behavior, you'd be right."

They all looked over at Andy Pettigrew, and he nodded.

"I agree. I'd also add that this narcissism, what I like to call a superiority complex, led him to think he was omnipotent, a godly controller of reality, thinking he could manipulate people and circumstances at will, meting out reward, and punishment to offenders like Dr. Waters. A serious miscalculation as it turns out."

"So the only reason to kill Rajput was to frame Dr. Waters for the murder," he said.

"Unless you have evidence I'm not aware of, yes," said Pettigrew.

Olivia and I were asked to wait until they'd finished with Billy in case new questions came up. The waiting room wasn't the height of luxury, but we were left alone. We talked about our interviews, which led to nothing disturbing. Olivia had described Erik's relationship with two cops who worked out of the nearest town, and the cozy dealings she'd often witnessed.

Having been around these types of interviews, I knew the detectives were alert for inconsistencies, and since we were all telling the truth, they saw none.

I took Olivia back to her house and volunteered to stay with her for a while, but she wanted to spend some alone time in her own home. She promised to set the burglar alarm.

On the way back to my condo, Santosan called to offer a heartfelt apology.

"You have taught me a lesson in humility," he said.

"Great. What was it?"

"I delved more deeply into the publicly available corporate records of ExciteAble. As a private company, this information is limited, but the effort bore fruit."

"Really."

"I would like to go over this with you," he said. "But not at the company."

"I'll come to you," I said.

"That would be most generous."

When I got to Rowayton, Santosan and his dog were waiting for me at a picnic table under a giant tree. He was back looking like he'd just flown in from Venice, California, and happier for it. On the table in front of him were a stack of file folders and a tablet device.

When I sat down, he said, "My job is to tell you what I've found. Your job is to listen, ask questions, and throw the tennis ball for the dog. Any direction you want. She's never failed to retrieve it."

"I had a dog like that once. I was just talking about her. Her world was a beat-up green rubber ball."

"I'm envious of such singularity of purpose," he said. "The absence of wanting anything more."

"That's doable," I said. "Just get certain portions of your prefrontal cortex removed. I know people who can do that."

"I'll consider it."

He opened the file on the top of the stack and gave thanks to Internet search engines, noting that the information once meant hours of poring through fat ledgers, files, and legal records in multiple locations acquired over weeks of struggle.

"Some say all that work made us better lawyers. To which I say bullshit, it made us exhausted lawyers with ruined eyesight."

He said, unfortunately, Google hadn't yet captured every scrap of data or piece of documentation in existence. Familiarity with the physical world was still essential.

"The robots don't own us yet," he said.

He described how he methodically traveled through a long list of public data bases. Nearly all of them government managed, and freely available.

"Contrary to conventional thinking, the government rarely hides the information it collects. The things they do try to bury get all the press, but that's a rare thing. Take patents, for example."

He said Google had a simple form you could use to search patents by a range of criteria. The more you knew, the quicker the search. Educated guesses, however, were unproductive, so it was better to plow through lots of patents that could be the target than try to narrow the effort with false criteria.

"And?" I asked.

"Paresh Rajput had a lot of patents. I made the mistake of starting with his first applications and moving toward the present. I learned that the closer we got to the present time, the more interesting things became. One of the criteria was the name of the assignee, the actual holder of the patent. For example, you could invent something and the assignee would be you personally. Or the inventor could be Dr. Waters and the assignee ExciteAble Technologies, since you developed your invention under their auspices."

"I get that."

"Until about two years ago, Paresh filed all his patents under ExciteAble as the assignee, making them corporate property. But then this other entity, PM Enterprises, LLC, shows up connected to Paresh, with a bunch of new patents. Who the hell is PM, I wonder."

"Totally separate from ExciteAble?"

"Totally. A distinct corporate entity," he said.

"Owned by?"

"Megan and Paresh. Sole shareholders. Their house is the corporate address."

"And all the patents filed for in the last two years went through this corporation," I said.

"Just a few. It looks to me like the most intricate and advanced technology, though I'm not an engineer."

"Give me the sexiest example."

"That's easy. It's a piece of avionics. You know what that is?" he asked.

"Systems that control an aircraft."

"This is an artificial intelligence-directed device that virtually eliminates pilot-caused disasters—takes over control of the aircraft and brings it safely back to earth when pilot decisions appear to be making bad calls, or intentionally trying to ditch the airplane. The end of terrorist pilots. The end of pilot error. The end of pilots. If it works."

"Did he get the patent?" I asked.

"He did."

"What would a thing like that be worth, assuming it works."

"Billions with a capital B," he said.

"And not an ExciteAble product."

"No. As far as I can tell, you, me, the patent office, and Megan Rajput are the only people who even know it exists. In our negotiations with Nelson Sarnac, the language is clear. He's purchasing all assets of ExciteAble Technologies, including gross receipts, production facilities, patents, and product portfolio. He's not buying everything invented by Paresh Rajput."

"So nothing about PM Enterprises."

"He doesn't know it exists. He could know, it's all in the public record, but you have to look. Like the *Purloined Letter*, it's hidden in plain sight. If he closes the deal, which can happen in a few weeks, he could try to sue Megan, but with no hope of winning. The law does not view shoddy due diligence as a legitimate defense."

The dog delivered the soggy ball and I carried it down to the harbor. She leaped at the hand carrying the ball, but I kept it aloft. She never let it leave her sight. When we got to the edge of the harbor I lowered the ball and asked if she wanted it. She responded by trying to grab it out of my hand, nearly taking a finger or two along with it. I sat down and let the ball just fall on the ground. The dog snatched it up, but then dropped it again. She looked up at me. I was missing the point. It was worthless without my intervention, my ability to animate the ball, turning it into a living creature worthy of the chase.

It wasn't about the ball. It was all about the game.

I threw the ball hard across the water, hard enough to assure a long swim for the dog, then went back to Santosan.

"I wouldn't tell anyone about this," I said, pointing to the files.

He gave a little bow.

"Not a chance of that," he said. "My fiduciary responsibility extends to ExciteAble, not Megan Rajput. The files will be on the boat when you need them."

Chapter Twenty-Eight

I'm a lousy salesman. I knew a lot about strategic selling, learned entirely from texts on the subject, which I used to develop training programs for our sales staff. I admired the skills of our engineers and administrative people, but I held particular esteem for the people in sales, who had an ability and temperament I found very rare and distinctive.

Anyone demeaning the profession had never tried to do it, or had tried, and failed. For me, the problem with selling was any sign of resistance. I could never get past what they thought were legitimate reasons for not buying the product or service. As soon as I understood the logic of their position, I'd capitulate. I could never convert those initial negatives into the very reason the customer needed to consider our offering.

"Of course you feel that way, which is exactly why you need to take a closer look at how we can address your specific issues," is what I taught our salespeople to say, but I never could.

I didn't think you could learn how to do that. It was a god's gift.

Yet I was faced with an important selling job only I could do, with very long odds of success. I needed to convince the staid, avuncular Fred Warner, a man of committed integrity and sternly held principles, to break in to his boss's house and violate the soul of technological honor and confidentiality.

I e-mailed him to ask for a meeting. The excuse was a routine training matter that would raise no suspicions. He gave me a time and date and I wrote back that we could meet in his office.

I loved that office. Spare to the point of monkish, tidy as a Zen rock garden, with the only decoration being two large, hand-rendered architectural drawings that he'd done when designing the house he and his wife had lived in for thirty years. I sat in the single visitor's chair and he loomed above his desk, in his usual white shirt and drab tie, a homely Gary Cooper playing Howard Roark with all the gravity and none of the bombast.

I told him the subject of the meeting was not as represented, and much more important. His reaction was somber.

"Okay, Dr. Waters. I'm all ears."

"A grave injustice may be about to happen. A deceit perpetrated on hundreds of people, causing financial wreckage and destroying the reputation of this company and everyone who works here."

"Jesus," he said. "What are you talking about?"

"How many new products has ExciteAble had in development in the last two years?" I asked.

"Maybe a half dozen."

"How innovative are they? How likely to move the company to another level?"

He looked both defensive and chagrined.

"Not likely. Small ball stuff. Mostly tweaks to existing technology."

"What if I told you the granddaddy of all game changers never made it into our product portfolio? The proverbial billion-dollar disruptor."

He folded his long arms across his chest and furrowed his majestic brows.

"I'd say you were speaking nonsense."

"But that's exactly what happened, and I can prove it, though only with your help."

He bowed his head and his shoulders sagged. I'd noticed people who had a hostile relationship with ambiguity, like Fred Warner, took unwelcomed news particularly hard.

"I've never had a coworker quite like you," he said. "I couldn't understand why Paresh brought you on as a full-time employee, this hard case from the casino who somehow managed to earn a doctorate. But over the years, I saw the value. Especially for the engineering department. Made my job a whole lot easier. So call me a convert."

"Thanks, Fred," I said. "We've worked well together."

"But you have to understand, I deal in the concrete world. Equipment either works as specified, or it doesn't. There's no room for politics, or subjective opinion. A lot of what happens outside the rules of science and engineering are a mystery to me, and frankly, somewhat deplorable. You've been a good buffer in that department."

I eased my chair closer to his desk.

"So you trust me," I said.

"No reason not to. So far."

"When you were a kid, did you ever do something you weren't supposed to do, but knew it was the better thing, and were happy you did it anyway?"

A faint hint of pride registered in his eyes.

"In high school, we did sneak into the computer room to run programs on a dumb terminal connected to the mainframes at Yale."

"Fred, that's what we're talking about here. The same exact thing."

"What are you proposing?" he said.

I described Paresh's basement R&D facility, how it looked no less advanced than the lab at ExciteAble, fully capable of producing industrial-grade prototypes. I knew I was on tenuous ground making these claims to the head of engineering, but I'd spent years learning about the technology we used in development and production, and I saw nothing spared in equipping Paresh's subterranean operation.

"Paresh started the company with products he designed in his basement," I said. "I don't think he ever stopped. Even when R&D was active here, he probably still worked on the basic concepts in his basement—designing, tweaking, and testing. Then for some reason, he stopped bringing the good stuff into work. It stayed in his basement."

Warner's deep bewilderment was not a hard read.

"But why?" he asked.

"I think I can figure that out if I can confirm one thing."

"What?"

"That one of the basement prototypes is what I think it is, and that it actually works," I said.

"How're you going to do that?"

"I'm not doing it. You are. We're going to break into Megan's house and you're going to determine if the prototype is operating according to the specs outlined in the patent."

Bewilderment turned to horror.

"Oh no, I'm not. No way in hell."

I pressed him for about a half hour, but it was clear nothing in the world would change his mind, that he'd rather sever a limb than commit a crime. In the midst of the debate, however, I had an idea.

"Fred, when I was down there with Megan, she checked a monitor that was plugged in to a bunch of test devices connected to the prototype. Then she gave it some coded instruction. She said it was Paresh's last project, and that it didn't work."

"That's a simulator. It sets the parameters of the test and aggregates all the data from the other gear. If I was going to do what you're asking me to do, which I'm not, I'd just bring along an external hard drive and download everything contained in the simulator—software, reporting, data—the whole shootin' match. Then bring it back to our computers here and analyze the results."

"That's it?"

"That's it," he said. "I'd just have to upload the simulator to one of our boxes, then have it run through diagnostics in the background while we did our other work."

I'd stumbled into one of the basics of good salesmanship. Start with the unachievable, then fall back to the possible.

"So if I get into the basement with a smartphone and video camera that shows you what I'm looking at, you can walk me through the download."

"Theoretically," he said.

"Come on, Fred. I'll set you up at my condo with a video monitor and phone connection. Untraceable to you. It's important."

"How important?"

"A matter of life and death. It's not often you get to say that and actually mean it. I'd prove it to you, but then you'd know things you wouldn't be able to keep to yourself."

He still looked fearful and wary, but a subtle shift in mood told me what those sales pros can read like large-type printing. I'd made the sale.

I had two days before I was sure Megan would be tied up at the office for at least a few hours. I spent some of that time testing the head-mounted camera and Internet link that sent a live feed to the desktop in my condo. I'd last used it in a Great Escape challenge where we had to prove we were following a strictly prescribed route. I'd paid our IT manager Bonnie Cardoni to set it all up, so it was just a matter of following her written instructions.

The other task was to harden Warner's wavering resolve, which took a lot more time and effort. One advantage was he'd already agreed once and found going back on a promise almost as bad as enabling a felony.

The day came when Megan was scheduled to be locked up with Nelson Sarnac, his lawyer, and Santosan working through the thicket of paperwork necessary for the acquisition. I asked Santosan to ping me if Megan left the building. He didn't ask why and I didn't tell him.

I greeted Fred Warner and led him to the desktop computer. I put on the head-mounted camera and showed him how to control the monitor, fairly simple and a pleasure for an engineer. I put the camera, a ten-terabyte hard drive, surgical gloves, a flashlight, and a short pry bar in a backpack and rode the motorcycle to a small park where I chained it to a tree. Then I walked a route that went through the woods behind Megan's house, and up to the back of the garage which had an access door. The first important question was about to be answered—did she have a security system? The last time I was there she didn't, as proven by the evening's gunfight. It would make sense to subsequently install at least a burglar alarm, but somehow I thought she hadn't bothered.

I used the pry bar to bust open the access door and waited for an alarm to go off. A silent alarm might already be waking up the guys at the security company, but I searched the door frame and around the garage and saw no evidence of alert sensors. So I just walked through the garage and down the stairs into Paresh's private paradise.

I called Warner at my apartment and was glad to hear his voice. I flicked on the camera and enabled the link with my smartphone. Minutes later he said I was live, describing what was right in front of me. I went over to the black box prototype and asked him what he saw.

"Interesting. Get a little closer to that device in the upper right with the silver faceplate. I can't quite make out the lettering." I read it to him. "That's what I thought. Just move through the other equipment, pointing to and reading whatever text or numbers appear stamped or printed you can make out."

Which I did.

"What is all this stuff?" I asked.

"Control systems. Everything you need to fly an airplane, including the standard autopilot. Either the actual devices or simulators. Can you get around behind the array?" When I did, he asked me to stand where the camera captured the whole system at the sharpest video resolution. "Important to know how it's wired," he said.

I went back around front and he had me follow the wiring from the keyboard stowed under the bench to what I guessed was a rack-mounted server. He told me where I might find a USB port, and he was right. I plugged in the external hard drive.

"Go back to the keyboard and I'll tell you what to do."

With patience earned over a long career, most of that training and directing others, Warner walked me through the sequence of downloading the software that ran the simulator, and all the data it captured. There were a few blind alleys he had to back me out of, but within about fifteen minutes I had a little window that said "Download."

A bar meter popped up and started to fill left to right.

"How long?" I asked.

"Probably at least an hour."

"Sorry. It's going to get boring. Feel free to switch to the ball game."

"I have a better idea," he said. "Walk around and let me record this whole facility. Professional curiosity."

"A much better idea. Here we go."

It was a fast hour. He directed my camerawork and occasionally asked me to read brand names, model and serial numbers. We filmed everything, including tools, the contents of drawers, the parts bins, even what was in the refrigerator, which included a freezer filled with microwaveable Indian cuisine. When we got to Paresh's sleeping area, we filmed inside two freestanding cabinets, one a chest of drawers, the other a closet, both fully stocked with shoes and clothing.

I heard a ding come from across the lab. I walked over there and pointed the camera at the monitor. Warner confirmed that the download was complete.

Seconds after that I got a text from Santosan that said their meeting was over, though it looked like Megan was heading for her office. He had to leave, so that was the best he could do.

"Time to boogie," I said to Warner.

"You're going to dance?"

"It's an expression, Warner. It means to briskly leave the premises. Flee. Bounce. Run away. Bug out."

I didn't actually boogie. I shut off the camera and went into the house, where I took a tour of the parts I hadn't seen the last time I was there. There were four bedrooms,

the master more of a suite, though no bed. It had been converted to a home office, with a large desk, computer station,
and file cabinets. As with the rest of the house, it was grace-
fully designed, with many home-like amenities, including a
row of hardwood bookcases and a seating area.

I sat at the computer desk. In addition to the keyboard
and screen, there was a full ashtray, empty wine glass, and
an old-fashioned daily planner that went back to the beginning of the year. It was in Megan's handwriting and full of
financial and corporate deadlines and reminders. I turned on
the computer, but it was password protected. So no go there.
I looked through the file cabinets, but without a few days for
the task, there was no point trying to search around. I noted
that most of the files also related to financial and corporate
matters.

The bathroom was all female. No men's shaving gear,
aftershave, or deodorant. One toothbrush. A tall cabinet full
of makeup, perfume, Q-Tips, creams, and other feminine
paraphernalia.

I left the bathroom and went over to the bookcases. Consistent with the theme, many of the titles dealt with business advice, strategy, and accounting. Biographies of business
heroes and famous political and military leaders. Nearly half
the books were fiction, with a fair representation of nine-
teenth- and twentieth-century classics.

One row that looked filled with matching book spines
was actually made up of photo albums. I sampled some of
them, showing Paresh and Megan on vacation, at family
gatherings, weddings, and company parties. They looked a
lot younger, so I searched for more recent photos, and came
across another slim album of shots taken somewhere in the
Caribbean. Palm trees, white sand, sailboats, and scenes at

funky bars. It was a trip with friends, taken maybe five years before. Very close friends. Megan was there, but no Paresh.

I slipped the album into my backpack and left.

On the way home, I stopped by the side of the road and called Warner.

"I'm coming," I said. "I just have one question. Does the simulator know it's been copied and downloaded?"

He thought about it.

"Probably, but you'd have to go look through the directories. It wouldn't just tell you the next time you logged on. Unless programmed to do so."

"What are the odds it was programmed?"

"I don't know. Fifty-fifty?"

I'd learned in statistics class that in probability theory, the most powerful theorist in the field was a man named Murphy, who stated that if something can go wrong, it probably will.

CHAPTER TWENTY-NINE

Fred Warner was ecstatic to get out of my condo, less so taking possession of the external hard drive. But he stuck to our agreement, and said he'd run it through an analytics tool that would do all sorts of things I didn't understand, so I made him say if he could tell me the prototype worked or didn't.

"Sure, I can do that, but it's still just a prototype," he said, and started to list other constraints and stipulations until I politely made him stop.

I taught a social skills course for engineers called, "How to Fool People into Thinking You're Normal." I drew wisdom from that, shook his hand, and said I looked forward to his analysis.

Shapiro called to say that Erik Humboldt's DNA matched Kozlowski's sample. Ballistics had matched the guns found in his hut in the Berkshires with rounds retrieved from the walls at my condo and Megan's house. They'd found the Plato ChatJazz account on his computer, though the conversations were still being extracted. And searches for "Home Made Cherry Bomb Bombs" and "10 Best GPS Trackers" were in his Google favorites.

"He's our man," I said.

"Oh, yeah. No question. We got a psych eval the NYPD did after that lethal force event that Pettigrew interpreted as a clear case of antisocial disorder. They let him leave with a clear record and full pension rights, so he could come up here to ply his wares in Connecticut. Nice job, NYPD."

I thanked him for the information, and for everything he'd done for me during the whole ordeal. I said it was above and beyond. Then I asked him one more thing.

"Where did Humboldt do that research you told me about?"

"On the desktop at his house, where he did all his work."

"Like at night, or early in the morning?"

"Geez, I don't know. I got the logs here from the investigation. Hold on."

I waited almost ten minutes for him to come back on the line.

"Sorry for the delay," he said. "Looks like he was pretty much 24/7. Bastard worked all hours of the night and day. I wish I had that kind of energy."

"No rest for the wicked."

Fred Warner didn't need the whole two days to decide on the functionality of Paresh Rajput's AI autopilot. He admitted to spending company time, and all his free time, running the analysis, and was as close to giddy over the results as a man like him could be.

"Brilliant, Waters," he said. "I always thought Paresh was a genius, but this thing is unbelievable. It actually learns the behavioral norms of the pilot and copilot, based on information collected by the flight recorders of any plane they've ever flown, matches them to their current inflight performance, and stands ready to take control if any irregularity appears, caused by the pilots or bad actors. The pilots' union will go nuts, but the airlines and regulators will lap it up."

I was pleased that he had a clear decision and disturbed by what it meant.

"Thanks, Fred," I said. "Capture your analysis and dump it on the external hard drive with everything else. Then scrub your system of anything connected to this thing. You can do that, right?"

"I can. What do I do with the hard drive?"

"I'll pick it up as soon as you tell me it's ready."

I didn't tell him I was bringing it to Los Umbros detective agency to hold for me.

His mood took a slight turn.

"I'm frightened, Waters, I admit it. This skullduggery is not a normal thing for me."

"You did a good deed, Fred. You're safe."

"I trust you," he said, as much a warning as a pronouncement.

I took the morning off to grab the hard drive from Warner, then sat in my condo to write a letter to Nelson Sarnac. My first draft was about ten thousand words, all of which I chose with great care. I printed it out and copied the document. Then I started paring it down, deciding what was absolutely necessary, and what could be left out. This wasn't an editing job for style, it was an exercise in organizing a story, making it tangible by seeing it on the screen, and then the printed page.

Sarnac didn't need the whole deal. For him, it ultimately boiled down to this: "The most valuable asset produced by Paresh Rajput is not in ExciteAble's patent portfolio. It's an invention which could be many orders of magnitude more valuable than all other properties combined."

Then I attached links to the PM Enterprises corporate registration, and their patents, beginning with the AI auto-pilot. I printed it out, then downloaded the letter and all previous drafts onto a flash drive and deleted them off my desktop. I took the letter to FedEx and sent it to Sarnac's home address, no signature required.

Then I went into the office.

———— • ————

IT ONLY took a day for Santosan to alert me that he was on his way over to ExciteAble for an emergency meeting with Megan, Sarnac, and his lawyer. I asked him about Megan's mood.

"I think rip-shit sums it up."

"You're in for a lively meeting," I said.

"For sure."

I spent that day on the plant floor doing routine follow-ups with various production teams. It was satisfying work, since few adjustments were needed, and morale seemed relatively high. The only exception being Chief Engineer Fred Warner, who called me into his office. Brice had told him Sarnac recently marched into the building, not looking too happy.

"You don't look well, Fred," I said.

"What does that mean?"

"I think you should take the rest of the day off."

He exposed a rainbow of complex emotions, more than you'd expect from a man with such an even temperament.

"I know what you're getting at," he said. "You think they'll call me in to answer technical questions and I'll buckle." I assured him that wasn't true. "It is. I understand, but you don't have to worry about me."

I said I believed him, because I did.

We shook hands and went separate directions.

On the way home I called Glen at Los Umbros and asked him to do another search for me. I'd been avoiding this, but one of the closed-off portions of my mind had been hammering on the door to be let out. I consoled myself by thinking it would decide the issue one way or the other. If it was good news, I could tell that little demon to shut the hell up and crawl back into its hole.

When I got to my condo, I opened the door, and punched the code into the security keypad to stop the irritating whine. At the moment it stopped, my face was smashed into the door and I was thrown against the foyer wall.

It was Megan's muscle, Carmine Fusco.

My eyes had just begun to focus when he smacked a heavy handgun across my face. I put up my hands to ward off another blow and he punched me in the abdomen. I was surprised at how much the blow took out of me. I lost my footing and fell to my knees and he punched me hard in the face. When I hit the floor, I curled in a ball, which only attracted kicks to my kidneys and the back of my head.

I saw a foot pass by my face and reached out to grab it. He tried to shake me off, but I lurched up on my knees and pulled hard, toppling him over onto his back. I tried to drag myself into a better fighting posture, but when I looked down at him he had the gun pointed at my face.

"I'm supposed to bring you in alive," he said. "But you're making it difficult."

"Bring me where?"

"Megan Rajput's house. She's eager to have a sit-down."

"You know, a simple invitation would have worked fine,"
I said.

"Not for the kind of sit-down she has in mind."

We rode in his giant SUV in silence. I knew it wasn't
worth asking him to tell me more, and small talk was out
of the question, given the circumstances. At a stoplight I
thought about jumping out of the truck, but there was a real
possibility he'd shoot me, stupid as that would be. I didn't feel
like taking another bullet just to test his relative intelligence.

When we got to Megan's house, he told me to walk ahead
of him and go straight through the door without knocking.
Inside, he said to go to the kitchen. Megan was waiting there,
sitting on a stool at the center island. Her elbows were on the
granite top, her hands clasped under her chin. Fusco had me
sit on the stool at the other end of the island and he stood
behind me.

"Sarnac has backed out of the deal," she said. "And you
know why."

"Sure. I told him to."

"I'm very disappointed in you, Waters," she said.

"That's too bad, because I'm very impressed with you."

"What did you do with it?"

"What?"

"The download from the simulator."

"Sorry, Megan, you need to be more specific."

"Go to hell, Waters."

"Are you sure you want Carmine to hear this conversation?"

"He's loyal to me, not like other people I know."

"I was loyal to you when I thought you deserved it. When
I was dealing with an alternative version of Megan Rajput.
She might not have been as smart as the genuine article, but
I liked her a lot better."

"How does it feel to play the fool?"

"Not as big a fool as Nelson Sarnac. He thought he got the better of you. Okay, he trimmed about sixty million off the price of ExciteAble, but he left about a billion on the table."

She looked over my shoulder at Fusco, gauging his reaction, probably wishing she'd taken my advice and asked him to leave.

"Even if what you say is true, and it's not, why do you give a shit what happens to the deal with Sarnac? The bastard used that psychopath Yolanda to set us up so he could swoop in and grab ExciteAble at a fire sale price. He was about to get what he deserved, and you decide to screw me instead. Metaphorically, since that's the best your limp dick could muster," she said.

Fusco cleared his throat. She slid a glance at him as if forced to recognize he was there.

"It wasn't Yolanda who moved that corporate money into my accounts. It was you. Paresh was so honest and disingenuous," I said. "One hundred percent engaged with the technology, oblivious to all business and administrative matters. That was your department. You never really left financial management as ExciteAble grew and took on staff. You just worked here at the house and stuck paperwork in front of Paresh to sign. Everything but technology flowed through you. That included establishing shell corporations and filing patents. And as we now know, moving patents from one entity to another. Nobody knew you'd locked up the AI autopilot with a completely different company."

I thought she might throw her glass at me, but I was ready to take the hit. Instead she spit, a valiant try, though it fell somewhere in the middle of the island.

"It's a damn shame Humboldt didn't get you when he had the chance," she said.

"When did you decide to go from framing me for Paresh's murder, to trying to scare me off, to actually trying to kill me for real?"

"What the hell does that mean?"

"A house in the south of France with hot and cold running gigolos?" I said. "What are the odds both you and Erik Humboldt would use that same bit? You knew each other, and well. Erik was the instrument, but you ran the controls."

I turned around so I could see Fusco's face for myself. He didn't look very comfortable. I stared at his eyes until he said, "What are you looking at?"

I turned back to Megan.

"You want me to keep going?" I asked her.

"No. I want you out of my house, and out of my company. If you set foot in there again I'll have you arrested. Carmine, give him a nice going-away present."

He took me by the shoulder, but I shook off his hand and started walking toward the door.

"Where do you think you're going?" he asked.

"I'm taking a cab," I said to him, looking down at my smartphone and tapping it with my thumb. When he followed me out of the house and down the drive, I turned around to show a picture of him in the kitchen holding a gun. "I've already got the text ready to send to the New Haven police. If you come at me, one push of a button and it'll be on its way."

As if by reflex he stowed the gun in the pocket of his jacket. In about the same time, I had my little automatic in my hand.

"You're in over your head," I said, pointing the gun at his face. "Get out of here before you drown."

And he did, I think relieved.

I went back into the house. Megan was still in the kitchen, nursing another big-girl drink of something on the rocks. And smoking a cigarette.

I pulled up a counter stool.

"Nobody knows what happens inside a relationship," I said.

"You got that right. Everybody loved Paresh. Lucky for them they didn't have to live with him."

"I saw his place in the basement."

"He never left it," she said. "Hadn't been in my bed for years. Do you know how humiliating that can be? I said we had to end the marriage, but he refused. Said if I even tried to leave, I'd get nothing. Yet I was still supposed to hide here in the house and run the business, be his lab technician and host parties for his friends and customers like a good little wifey."

"It's all going to unravel, you know that," I said. "No matter how careful you were, it's impossible these days to hide what you've been up to. Once they know where to look."

She took a solid pull off her drink.

"We'll see about that."

"We will."

CHAPTER THIRTY

I was walking out of Megan's neighborhood heading for a commercial strip, where I felt safer waiting for a cab, when I got a call from Glen at Los Umbros.

"I have something for you," he said.

I asked if he could come pick me up.

"Sure. Be there in a few minutes."

"Can you tell me what it's about?" I asked.

"I can, but I'd rather show you. And brace yourself. You're not going to like it."

Bad news withheld. One of my favorite things.

On the way to his office he filled the dead air with talk about the Boston Red Sox, a subject about which I knew absolutely nothing. But I'm good at active listening, so it gave us something to do.

As he unlocked the door to let us into their office, he started to explain.

"I did the search like you asked me to," he said. "This isn't going to be fun."

He took me into his personal office and gave me a chair in front of the desk. He went around and sat at the desk in front of the computer. He told me to give him a second to boot up and make the proper link.

He said, "If it wasn't kind of an important thing to know, I wouldn't bother you with this."

"Hey, Glen, just show it to me."

"Okay, boss."

He spun the computer around. First he showed me the cover of a high school yearbook. Saint Bridget's Academy, the all-girls Catholic high school for gifted students. The next shot was a photo and caption. The photo was a little fuzzy, but the text was clear enough to read.

"I got more stuff like it, but you get the picture," he said.

I did. I got the picture. In fact, I got the whole movie. We stared at each other in silence, with our own versions of the story playing in our heads. Though likely more or less the same.

"You had to know at some point," he said.

I shook my head.

"Not really."

"I got more," he said. "If you want."

I said sure, and he pulled up a scan of a police report. It was written by the detective who was first on the scene the night Erik Humboldt shot the guy who was abusing an escort. The language was in the flat, empirical, bureaucratic cop-talk we're used to hearing, but the writer was clearly uncertain about the situation as reported.

He wondered why the dead man was propped up on the backboard of a bed, naked. Why the entry wound was on his left side, when he was facing the door through which Humboldt said he entered. On the other hand, he reported the escort was clearly battered, with contusions showing on her face and defensive wounds up and down her arms.

The recordings leading up to the incident were clear that the perpetrator was assaulting the escort, with the intent of doing serious bodily harm.

However, he thought it was unfortunate that Detective Humboldt had switched off the recording device before racing to the escort's rescue and had failed to call in backup until after the encounter had taken place. He also noted that Detective Humboldt was not equipped with a handheld radio, being only tasked with surveillance, and understandably focused on saving a person's life.

"You ready?" said Glen, when I was finished reading.

"For what?"

"One more scan."

It was a series of photographs, taken by the ME of the dead assailant, and two standard front and side mug shots of his victim, the escort, booked on prostitution charges.

Her face was pretty banged up, but hardly unrecognizable.

"Can you take me to my condo?" I asked.

He started saying he was sorry again, but I shut him up and asked him to get me home. This time there was no desultory chatter, about the Boston Red Sox or anything else.

When we got there, I watched him drive away, then got on the motorcycle and took off into the night. A change in wind direction had made it a cool late-summer night, with dry air and clear skies. As usual, I kept off the four-lane roads and drove extra miles to my destination. I didn't mind since it gave me a kinder ride and more time to think.

That night on the motorcycle, I got to dwell on the totality of human experience—registering my error of judgment, and this time feeling the overwhelming sorrow that can come from allowing your heart to overrule your mind.

I parked the motorcycle a block down from Olivia's house and walked the rest of the way to her door. She answered, wearing a baggy sweat suit, her hair pulled back in a loose ponytail, a look I'd never seen.

"Waters," she said, "what the heck? Did you tell me you were coming over?"

I said I hadn't and walked past her into the house. The TV was on in the living room. I took the remote off a side table and turned it off, then dropped down into one of her fluffy sofas. I saw a wine bottle and half-full glass on the opposite side table and asked if she could pour me one of my own. As she went to get another glass I looked around the room, again marveling that people knew how to assemble physical things in such a pleasant way.

After she handed me my drink, she flopped down in the opposite sofa and said, "To what do I owe this pleasure."

"You look great," I said.

She laughed, "I've never looked worse."

"You're right. I've never seen you without makeup and nice clothes, your hair done just right. A type of fantasy woman, actually. But you didn't have to go to that much trouble. I would've liked you this way just as much."

"Strange way of putting it."

"I know everything," I said.

She cocked her head.

"Everything? Everything in the entire world?"

"About you and Megan and Erik with a K."

"Who's Megan?"

"Your BFF, according to your high school yearbook."

Her eyes narrowed, as if trying to get me into clearer focus.

"And what about Megan and me?" she asked.

"You two arranged for the murder of Paresh Rajput, conspired to pin his death on me, and set the stage for the death of Erik Humboldt. Excellent teamwork, by the way, which I'm professionally qualified to say."

She swirled the wine in her glass, trying to appear both angry and confused, but doing a bad job of it.

"Give me one good reason why I shouldn't throw you out of this house, you freak," she said.

I took the gun out of my rear waistband and put it in my lap.

"Because if you move from the sofa, I'll shoot you. That's what freaks do."

She shrunk into herself but had the poise to take a sip of wine, with steady hands.

"I've never heard such a ridiculous thing in my entire life," she said.

I answered that by telling the story of two old friends who stayed in touch after high school. One of them had hooked up with an Indian tech genius, the other fallen in with a bad crowd, or just went bad herself, becoming a high-priced female escort, a hooker by any other name. Something bad happened in the midst of this pursuit, enough to propel her into a new career, with the aid and support of her rescuer, an NYPD cop-turned PI.

Megan had the motivation, overall concept, cunning, and flair for theatrics. But Olivia had the wherewithal to pull it off, beginning with a devoted husband with both the skills and ruthless malice necessary to murder Paresh and set me up as the killer. It was the perfect match.

What they didn't allow for was Yolanda. A dark horse inserted by Nelson Sarnac. His plan was to sabotage the company in a way that only he could undo, allowing him to buy it for a drastically reduced price. Yolanda went in and did the dirty work, and then ran out of there, and Sarnac only had to drop a dime to his friends at the DOD.

To all of us this looked like disaster, but Megan knew she didn't really need ExciteAble if the patents she owned for the next wave of products were outside the company. The most important of which was the AI autopilot system.

Along the way, Megan, Olivia, and Erik made key changes to their strategy. Instead of trying to frame me, or scare me away, they decided to just kill me and be done with it. But this didn't work out so well either. When Mike Wojcik failed to beat me to death with a baseball bat, Erik decided to do it himself, but luck got in the way. Meaning, he missed. Megan tried to make it easier for him by inviting me to her house for dinner, but my Los Umbros guardian angel screwed that up.

The last gasp effort was to lure me to the Quonset hut in Vermont, but that obviously didn't work out so well either. Though it fulfilled Olivia's hope that she could take care of her Erik with a K problem, which wasn't over-possessiveness. It was the real possibility he'd be charged with Rajput's murder, and buy himself some leeway by incriminating his two female partners.

"By then, I was pretty sure you were in on it, I just didn't want to believe it," I said. "You might even say I willfully ignored my better instincts."

"You'll never prove any of this," she said. "You know that, don't you?"

I told her about the photo album Megan kept of her trip to the islands with Erik and Olivia, and the shot with Megan in their yearbook, arm-in-arm, best friends forever.

"There's plenty more where that came from. Detective Shapiro will get there. As I told your friend Megan, now that he knows where to look. Speaking of which, I'll be taking your laptop."

As with Megan, I'd lost all trust in my ability to divine Olivia's thoughts or feelings. Though maybe the only thing left in her heart and mind was fear.

Chapter Thirty-One

The FBI didn't have to follow through on their subpoena with ChatJazz. Having access to Megan, Erik, and Olivia's computers, cyber forensics was able to retrieve their respective ChatJazz accounts, and the correspondence they exchanged with each other, most of it damning.

Forensics also revealed that Paresh was probably killed in Megan's Mercedes, from a blow to the back of the head. From there, he was driven to my storage unit, where Olivia let them in, having learned the code from our frequent dalliances, and the dismemberment commenced. Whether the women stuck around for that part or not would never be known. Both held to their innocence all the way to the state penitentiary with matching twenty-five-years-to-life sentences.

Yolanda's death remained officially accidental. Whether it was Erik and his partners, or Nelson Sarnac, who did the deed, was immaterial to me. The world was better off without her.

Losing our family dog was the worst thing that had happened to me until my brother left me a note announcing his decision to disappear into the woods and try to drink and drug himself to death. This brought a depth and breadth of suffering that was unimaginable. A few weeks later, they found his car, and a bagful of empty bottles, but not his body. Eventually, they declared him dead, which everyone but me came to accept.

So I had a gauge for the level of bottomless grief one can feel. Though the combined loss of Paresh, Megan, and Olivia would never reach those depths, there was still ample sadness to absorb.

I'd been taught that it was possible to divine human behavior, if you took your time and trusted the science. My brother's disappearance killed that belief in me, if it had ever really taken hold. I loved him too much to really know him, and his actions remained as inexplicable as the mind of the divine. Shakespeare knew better, that love is blind and lovers cannot see. And for me, whenever love got involved, the beloved disappeared.

When they announced the convictions, I resigned from ExciteAble and left them with the impending legal fight between Nelson Sarnac and Paresh's family over the company and its assets, including the AI autopilot.

I bought an SUV, packed it full of Great Escape gear, and drove it into the woods to the spot where they found the last trace of my brother. I didn't know if I'd be looking for a skeleton or a ghost, or maybe something far better, if hope was more than illusion. He might've given up on his life, but he was the one who convinced me, all those years ago, that loss is not destiny. No matter how difficult, the game is worth playing.

Acknowledgments

D_{r.} Mark Braunsdorf provided much of the inspiration and professional information on the activities of corporate psychologists. To my knowledge he does not ride motorcycles or shoot high tech pistols, but there's always time to start. Ron Perine, CEO of Mintz + Hoke, taught me much of what I know about business accounting, most of which I've failed to retain. Tim Hannon, hospitality expert, advised on hotel features and procedures, and vulnerabilities.

Eric Knight, inventor, guided me through the patent process.

Captain Chris Chute of the Waterbury, CT, police department, instructed me on criminal interviews and interrogations, at the end of which I was ready to confess.

Saikat Majumdar and his friends Bittu, Alex, and Ravindran Sriramachandran cleared my Indian names. Jill Fletcher helped out with the New Britain neighborhood. Dave Newell did the same for the hills of Vermont.

Special thanks to Jill Fletcher and Barbara Anderson for sticking with me through multiple revisions, above and beyond the call. Other editorial advice came from Dan Pope, Lynn Wilcox, and Marjorie Drake.

Permanent Press co-publishers Marty and Judy Shepard continue to take their chances with me, as does my wife, Mary Farrell.